Half a Day for Caste?

AF512278

D. Veeraraghavan (1958–2009) studied history
in Chennai at R.K.M. Vivekananda College, Presidency College,
and Pachaiyappa's College. In 1982 he joined IIT Madras for
his PhD and submitted his thesis, in 1987, on the history of the
working-class movement in interwar Chennai. The next year
he joined its faculty and taught there until his premature death.
His *The Making of the Madras Working Class* (LeftWord, 2013)
was published posthumously to wide acclaim.

A.R. Venkatachalapathy, historian and Tamil writer,
is a professor at the Madras Institute of Development Studies
(MIDS), Chennai.

Half a Day for Caste?

Education and Politics in Tamil Nadu, 1952–55

D. VEERARAGHAVAN

Edited by

A.R. VENKATACHALAPATHY

LeftWord

First published in January 2020
Reprinted January 2023

LeftWord Books
2254/2A Shadi Khampur
New Ranjit Nagar
New Delhi 110008
INDIA

LeftWord Books is the publishing division of
Naya Rasta Publishers Pvt. Ltd.

© Dr Dilip Veeraraghavan Memorial Trust, 2019

leftword.com

ISBN 978-81-943579-0-2

Printed and bound by Chaman Enterprises, Delhi

CONTENTS

Abbreviations 9

FOREWORD 11
by Gopalkrishna Gandhi

EDITORIAL PREFACE 17

'DILIP' VEERARAGHAVAN (1958–2009) 21

PROLOGUE
The Controversy in Context 27
by A.R. Venkatachalapathy

HALF A DAY FOR CASTE?

INTRODUCTION 57

CHAPTER I
The Genesis of the Scheme 61

CHAPTER II
Launch, Implementation, and Reaction 83

CHAPTER III
The Second Round of Battle 115

CHAPTER IV
The Climax and After 129

CONCLUSION 149

Bibliography 151

Index 159

ABBREVIATIONS

Central Advisory Board of Education	CABE
Dravidar Kazhagam	DK
Dravida Munnetra Kazhagam	DMK
Director of Public Instruction	DPI
Periyar E.V. Ramasamy	EVR
Indian Administrative Service	IAS
Member of Legislative Assembly	MLA
Member of Legislative Council	MLC
Member of Parliament	MP
Modified Scheme of Elementary Education	MSEE
Parulekar Committee Report	PCR
E.V. Ramasamy	Periyar
C. Rajagopalachari	Rajaji
South India Teachers' Union	SITU
Secondary School Leaving Certificate	SSLC
Tamil Nadu Congress Committee	TNCC
United Nations Educational, Scientific and Cultural Organization	UNESCO

FOREWORD

Gopalkrishna Gandhi

Rajaji was conservative.

That, to borrow a part-phrase he coined, was the A to Z of his politics, his life.

Being conservative meant, to him, conserving what he found to be valuable. Had linguistics, not politics, been his field he would have been an etymologist. Had architecture, not the legislature been his site of action, his metier would have been the repair and restoration of grace in built heritage. Had weaving at a loom, not arguing in court, been his profession, he would have flown the shuttle to revive old patterns using vegetable, not chemical dyes, to create contrasts in the warp, conjunctures in the weft.

What he wanted to, chose to, and tried to conserve was of course determined by his own choice-processes. The conserver and conserved were in compact. That would have caused no problem or difficulty to anyone or to any stage in the history of his society except for the fact that his stars led him to seats of influence or authority where his conservation choices became the ingredients for policy and, indeed, policy itself. Is this not how any policy gets determined—that is, from the propulsion of an individual's mind? So it does, but in a few people like Rajaji, whose faith in his own judgment was much stronger than his trust in the judgment of others, this subjectivity, even when of the most un-questionable probity and intent can become authoritarian. Rajaji's conservatism, whenever it was empowered by position or office, turned from being a strong attitude to becoming a stern advocacy. And its 'allies' were not what they should have been, namely, prudent consultation or reflective discussion but an exclusivist dependence on the powers of his own intellection, his own exposition. He was the master and slave of his own argumentative sparkle.

Rajaji was also innovative. That, to borrow another part of the same phrase of his, meant that stagnation was his enemy number one and he was stagnation's enemy number one. An ideational restlessness kept his conservative mind in constant ferment. This ferment was in its own way, innovatively intellectual, innovatively creative. 'Schemes' and 'formulas' emerged from his fertile mind with speed and force. Spoken and written advocacy being his metier. As with any innovation, the appeal of originality worked on him. And this attraction to the original included an original reconsideration of his own conservatism. This is where his early encountering of another conservative-innovator, M.K. Gandhi, made this innovative trait or tendency in him more than a style of functioning. It made it his signature in action. And the *charkha*, Gandhi's spinning wheel, was its most symbolic and most stellar 'key'. The *charkha*, like the loom, was an old, a very old, appliance of daily livelihood. Ergo, it fitted into a conservative's and rural idealizer's mindscape effortlessly. The *charkha* was something anyone with two wrists and ten digits for fingers—young, old, rich, poor, urban. rural, 'high' caste or 'low' caste—could, without too much training or expense, ply to make a point—Swadeshi—and break a spell—imperial hubris. And its product, a length of white cotton, was something which seemed to have a length of pristine power. Hand-spinning and its kin, hand-weaving, became for Rajaji the craft co-relative of intellectual creativity.

Rajaji's conservatism and innovativeness had, as they did with Gandhi, a kindred spirit—frugality. This came from the insufficiently known circumstance of his financial straits. When his *munsiff* father earning Rs 5 a month sent Rajan to Bangalore to study, he had to sleep on the floor of a choultry in Chickpet, spending a grand sum of Rs 2 a month on that luxury. Before thrift and simplicity became for him a preferred personal style, they were an ineluctable reality. Conserving and contrivance were for him the hand-me-downs of inherited financial stringency as much as they were a natural bent. He was indigent by material circumstance before he became provident by intellectual labour. But in all this, severely, alone.

As a conservative he acted individually. As an innovator he acted distinctively.

When, after the elections in 1952, the Indian National Congress's legislative party in Madras found itself facing ouster from office and a Communist government replacing its own, it turned to him for leadership. He complied, both as a conservative and an innovator. The conservative in him wanted to contribute to the stalling of a Communist takeover, albeit wholly democratic, of the state's government. The innovator in him wanted to use the chance that had come unexpectedly his way, to turn some Gandhi-inspired projects of his own ideation into state policy. He had done that, some twelve years earlier, during his first helming of the province's government. On that earlier occasion, as premier, the powers he held and the influence he exercised were, despite the restrictiveness of the Government of India Act of 1935, extensive. Quite overwhelming the British Governor and civil servants of the day by his intellectual sparkle and his propensity for hard work, he was premier in every sense of the term. Now, in 1952, with a very different wind blowing over his new-old office and the new-old legislative assembly hall in Madras's Fort St George, the former Premier, Union Minister, Governor and Governor-General was in for a surprise.

The distinctive individuality of the former Premier was out of joint in times when as a chief minister he was answerable if not accountable to popularly elected MLAs, to his own party bosses and to a party high command and government at the Centre. An exclusive thinker's whimsy, howsoever exalted in intent and elevated in tone, is in a democratic scheme subject to more than the standards of his own. It is subject to the judgment of a wider, diverse constituency called 'public sentiment'. This his lean and lone intellect could not grasp.

D. Veeraraghavan's treatise, set within the editorial casing of A.R. Venkatachalapathy's thoughts, tells the story, piquant and plangent, of how Rajaji's very 'own' scheme for a re-orientation of elementary education in the state collapsed, like a tiny runnel formed by a chance shower gets absorbed without trace in the surge of a river in its flood.

The late Veeraraghavan has written with a clear disposition against the failed scheme's arbitrariness and its philosophical pre-suppositions robustly but without prejudice against its inceptor. He has thereby shown to us, in essence, the limitations of an individual leader's prerogatives in the assemblies of popular representation.

Rajaji's self-containment and parleying insufficiency was unfortunate as such but also supremely imprudent. If he had taken the scheme's adversaries into confidence at an early stage of their demurring, some ideas could have emerged that might have purged the scheme of its unintentional distortions, especially the effect of caste-perpetuation, and saved both the scheme and his chief ministership. Someone might have suggested to him, if only he had given those 'someones' the time, that curricular learning or 'book' learning has to be the school's central and un-diluted core, and instead of 'parental' or 'traditional' or 'customary' crafts, the new second vocational shift should concentrate, across communities, on hand-spinning and weaving and on the making and maintaining of progressively improved tools of agriculture, husbandry and animal rearing, with a research and development aspect. Also, that there is something called sport, fun. Children could be made to read and to put their hands to work. But what of the joy of their sporting spirit? That should be factored in. The argument might have worked with someone who was once 'thin-faced eagle-nosed Rajan', with defective eyes whose being 'specky' made swimming—a natural preoccupation in villages—impossible but who learnt some wrestling holds from a young Muslim boy, who was as devoted as Rajan was to a rock-carved Hanuman on the red-earth flatness of Hosur. None of this—*khadi*, husbandry-crafts, sports—could have been faulted by *khadi*-wearing Congress men or 'development'-minded legislators of any mould. But did he listen? Did he ask? He knew what was best and that was that! Veeraraghavan brings out Rajaji's mental chemistry with the sharpness of a psychoanalyst.

In his recounting and analysis, the historian in Veeraraghavan has balanced, with the Euclidean precision of a scale's needle, his own ideological affinity and sense of egalitarian veracity with the intent of the scheme's conservative formulator. He has in plain prose taken on something of a playwright's sense of narrative give-and-take, investing every major player in the enactment his own space, his own moment. I say 'his', here, choicelessly for one of the verities emerging from this narrative is the almost total absence in it of the female voice except in the passive though 'equal' presence of the girl-child in the school systems being discussed.

In times when democratic norms are under threat—not from an independent thinker's impulsive stubbornness but from manipulation by supremacist agendae—one may read of Rajaji's educational scheme with nostalgia for times of political innocence when an honest administration's offence was compliance before a chief minister's whimsicality, a chief minister's failing was arbitrariness, and a storm-tossed legislative assembly's greatest moment lay in jettisoning the very distinctive lifeboat on which its majority had returned to its 'regular ship' cruising on the calm waters of stability.

Chennai
Tamil New Year Day
14 April 2019

EDITORIAL PREFACE

This book is based on D. Veeraraghavan's MPhil dissertation, 'Modified Scheme of Elementary Education of Madras State in the Year 1953 and Its Impact'. The research was carried at Pachaiyappa's College, Chennai during the academic year 1980–81, and the degree was awarded by the University of Madras soon after. Veeraraghavan himself never kept a copy of the dissertation and, apart from publishing a small fragment on the genesis of the scheme in a souvenir, avoided discussion about it. Shortly after his death in early 2009, V.R. Muraleedharan (Muralee) and I launched a search for it. Despite the help of many friends, the final dissertation copy could not be traced either in the college where he studied or in the university which awarded the degree. The family of his supervisor too did not have a copy. Such, alas, is the state of India's higher education. Fortunately, the late S.S. Kannan, Veeraraghavan's mainstay and benefactor, managed to fish out an uncorrected, messy, carbon copy of the first draft from his miscellaneous papers. But as luck would have it, the first (introductory) chapter was not to be found.

For whatever reason, Veeraraghavan was disconcerted by his work and avoided all discussion about it. But a quick reading of the surviving draft easily confirmed my suspicion that it was no embarrassing juvenilia. The study is based on a thorough exploration of the relevant sources: government reports; legislative assembly and council debates; a range of contemporary periodicals (both in English and Tamil); biographies and memoirs; and a vast body of secondary literature on the history of education and educational philosophy. Apart from this enviable set of sources, Veeraraghavan had met and interviewed many of the actors in the drama of the 1950s. The only source not consulted was the proceedings (Government Orders) of the Government of Madras. This was no failing but the result of the thirty-year rule of access to public archives. As the research had been conducted in 1980–81, the government files of 1950 and after were closed to researchers then.

Meticulous archival research apart, Veeraraghavan's analysis is characterized by considerable insight. Despite his age (he was barely twenty-three then), Veeraraghavan's understanding of the history of (especially Gandhian) educational ideas, the course of the national movement, the various streams within the Congress party, the political and social processes unfolding in south India, etc. is more than impressive.

Nearly four decades after its drafting, there is no study that has superseded Veeraraghavan's. That is the rationale for the publication of this book. A new study would have to cover the same archival ground again which would amount to reinventing the wheel. However, it would also be pointless to publish the study with a chapter missing. Having lost all hope of retrieving the final thesis, I decided to supply the missing bit. Through cross references and allusions in the text, it was easy to figure out the ground that Veeraraghavan had covered in it. I have also used memoirs and other material that have subsequently come to light (such as the reminiscences of C. Subramaniam and N.D. Sundaravadivelu, and the collected writings of Kalki R. Krishnamurthy on the question of education which includes many of the essays that Veeraraghavan cites from the original *Kalki*). I hope my background chapter does justice to Veeraraghavan's study and helps the reader better appreciate the narrative and the analysis.

Given the thoroughness with which Veeraraghavan consulted the sources it would be a shame for the book to be published without taking into account the government files which are now open. I have therefore consulted the over fifty government files concerning the Modified Scheme of Elementary Education lodged in the Tamil Nadu Archives.

While they yielded some supplementary information, there was little that altered the narrative of events or the analysis. I have therefore incorporated additional information derived from the files in the footnotes and, in a few cases, where appropriate, in the text itself. In all cases, the insertions have been clearly flagged—being placed in square brackets or indicated as such in the references. Minor additions have been made to provide details on the personalities discussed. I have also polished the text for grammar, style, and consistency. This has been done, hopefully, without violence to the intent, argument, or emphasis of the author. As far as possible I have checked references and supplied missing bibliographical details. I imagine Veeraraghavan would have approved of all the changes made with the reader in mind.

The book has been long overdue. Muralee and I first focused on bringing out Veeraraghavan's classic work on the history of the Madras working class in the first half of the twentieth century: *The Making of the Madras Working Class* (New Delhi: LeftWord, 2013). This book too has been made possible by the unstinting support of Muralee. Having full faith in me, he has supported the project wholeheartedly. His careful reading of the manuscript was a bonus. V. Rajesh spent much time in a vain effort to trace the thesis, and also facilitated the word processing of the text. K.A. Manikumar and S. Thillainayagam helped with the proofs. As usual, A. Arivazhagan helped in cleaning up the word files. S. Kokilavani provided crucial research assistance. Grateful thanks are due to Ms Seetha Ravi for permission to access the *Kalki* archive where S. Kumarselvam provided excellent assistance. The Periyar Rationalist Library and Research Centre, and the Tamil Nadu Legislative Assembly Library kindly permitted access to their holdings. J. Balasubramanian helped in tracking down many references. Aditya Balasubramanian—*the* Rajaji expert of the new generation—gave the manuscript the benefit of his critical reading.

Sudhanva Deshpande and Vijay Prashad enthusiastically accepted the book for publication. Nazeef Mollah did an excellent job of copy-editing the manuscript, apart from compiling the index.

Special thanks are due to Gopalkrishna Gandhi for reading the manuscript closely, offering comments, and writing a perceptive foreword.

It is a lasting regret that S.S. Kannan did not live to see this book.

A.R. VENKATACHALAPATHY — Chennai, 23 March 2019

'DILIP' VEERARAGHAVAN (1958–2009)

A.R. Venkatachalapathy

The Madras Labour Union, founded in April 1918, was the first organized labour union in India. It was in Napier's Park, Madras, in 1923, that the May Day, led by M. Singaravelu Chettiar, was first celebrated in India. These are well-attested facts in the histories of the labour movement in India. But there was no coherent account of the labour movement in Madras until D. Veeraraghavan's book, *The Making of the Madras Working Class*, appeared in 2013. Posthumously published, it was based on a doctoral thesis titled 'The Rise and Growth of the Labour Movement in the City of Madras and its Environs, 1918–1939', submitted to the Indian Institute of Technology Madras in 1987.

Veeraraghavan's study relied on an exhaustive study of the voluminous documents in the colonial archive lodged in the Tamil Nadu Archives, Chennai. This was supplemented by research in the National Archives of India and other detailed reports produced by the colonial government. In addition to this, Veeraraghavan made extensive use of contemporary newspapers such as *The Hindu*, *New India*, *Swadesamitran*, and *Navasakthi*. He unearthed the *Swadharma*, the first periodical exclusively devoted to labour issues in India, and exploited to the full his access to leading labour and Communist leaders including G. Selvapathy Chetty, C.S. Subramaniam, P. Ramamurthi, V.P. Chintan, K. Murugesan, Gajapathy and others. Some of the records that he consulted have also since been lost. And even by the time of his search, the records in the Buckingham and Carnatic Mills had been swept away in a major flood in 1976. Nevertheless, the sheer documentary foundation on which his book is based alone makes it worthwhile; his analysis is a bonus. *The Making of the Madras Working*

Class remains the indispensable analytical and narrative record of this movement.

Veeraraghavan was no dry, careerist historian. Steeped in the Left movement, the choice of his research topic derived from political commitment. Well versed in the Marxist classics, he was also thoroughly read in labour history. His knowledge of the minutiae of the history of the Communist Party and its ideological strands and internal differences could be quite dazzling. Understandably, he was drawn to the British Marxist historians but his thesis was more influenced by Jean Chesneaux, the French historian of the Chinese working class, than by E.P. Thompson. In that vein, however unfashionable it may now be, Veeraraghavan's book is animated by a deep faith in the revolutionary potential of the working class.

Veeraraghavan wrote little. He was diffident about writing and consequently published few papers. His MPhil thesis, on which this book is based, went unpublished in his lifetime. It is a mature and politically informed study of an episode that marks a watershed in the history of independent Tamil Nadu, namely Rajaji's infamous '*kula kalvi*' scheme which mandated that primary school students spend half a day learning their father's hereditary trade.

I first got to know Veeraraghavan in 1984, upon entering the musty corridors of the Tamil Nadu Archives for the first time. If the writings in the colonial archives excited me, I found the discussions at the plebeian canteen sipping cups of milky tea even more exhilarating. Back then, the research hall teemed with scholars ranging from the septuagenarian co-founder of the Communist Party in Tamil Nadu C.S. Subramaniam, then carrying out a study of M.P.T. Acharya, to college teachers, doctoral students, and independent scholars. An especially active group was the doctoral students from the department of humanities and social sciences of IIT Madras. All of them, mentored by S. Ambirajan, worked on the interwar period. Ambirajan had just returned from the University of New South Wales. He was deeply dissatisfied with the interwar period research being produced in the West and Australia. Ambirajan perceived an imperialist slant to this research and made it his agenda to correct this. Veeraraghavan approached this period through the study of labour struggles in Madras city. His contemporary, T. Thankappan, worked on labour in other parts of Tamil Nadu.

Veeraraghavan seldom joined us as we chatted and debated in the canteen. He remained huddled in a corner poring over piles of documents of the Government of Madras. Since he paid a research assistant from his modest stipend, his reluctance to join us for tea was quite understandable. Veeraraghavan was blind and depended heavily on assistance. The statement of this disability is only a matter of fact and is no invitation to concession. He was the first visually challenged person to acquire a doctoral degree in Tamil Nadu. While he was in the forefront of struggles for the rights of the differently-abled, he detested patronizing and gratuitous praise. His curiosity and memory were unparalleled among his peers. By any reckoning his doctoral thesis is one of the finest produced in the social sciences in the last many decades in this part of the country.

Veeraraghavan was born on 8 October 1958 in an orthodox Iyengar family in Kumbakonam. Symptoms of retinitis pigmentosa were diagnosed at an early age. An incurable ailment, he gradually lost his sight and by the time of his school final had lost all vision.

Veeraraghavan then moved to Chennai where he completed his BA (History) at the R.K.M. Vivekananda College (1975–78), MA (History) at the Presidency College (1978–80), and MPhil at Pachaiyappa's College (1980–81). In 1982 he joined IIT Madras for a PhD and submitted his thesis in 1987. The next year he joined its faculty and taught there until his death.

It was in his college student days that Veeraraghavan was introduced to Marxism. Active in the Students' Federation of India, he was close to the Communist Party of India (Marxist) and maintained good relationships with party leaders ranging from P. Ramamurthi to Prakash Karat. He attended party and workers' meetings and taught theoretical classes. During his later years, however, he developed a distance mainly because of his changed position regarding environmental issues. The break-up of the Soviet Union took its toll, and he was ill at ease with the way the party coped with this debacle.

The social sciences and humanities were a poor cousin in the IITs, and technology students often used to put up with courses in them as a necessary evil. An inspiring teacher, Veeraraghavan weaned away a number of students from technology and engineering. Many of those who went on to become technocrats were sensitized to social issues. Students were fond of him, and many of them donated considerable sums of money which he used for various charitable educational purposes.

When one speaks of Veeraraghavan, one name comes to mind instantly. S.S. Kannan (1923–2017), a committed Marxist and founder of the Karl Marx Library, nurtured Veeraraghavan. The cornerstone of Veeraraghavan's life from his student days, Kannan played a central role in promoting the younger scholar's research and writing. Enriching his library with important acquisitions primarily for Veeraraghavan's benefit, Kannan also helped him in the writing of the thesis. Later, despite his advanced age, he brought out its Tamil version. He deeply regretted that Veeraraghavan did not continue his history of the Madras working class even though all the source material for the 1940s had been collected.

Veeraraghavan was a great music aficionado and would spend hours listening to Carnatic music. He was a regular in the Chennai music concerts and, as the music historian V. Sriram once remarked, few among the concert-going fans knew of his academic accomplishments. It is my lasting regret that he did not write a social history of Carnatic music.

Veeraraghavan maintained indifferent health all his life. A poor eater, he also suffered from juvenile rheumatoid arthritis. He belonged to a strand in the Indian Left which aspires to a Gandhian austerity. Though he could have easily afforded a car he insisted on taking public transport. A year before his death Veeraraghavan was diagnosed with tuberculosis of the large intestine. After pumping him with a cocktail of drugs doctors changed their diagnosis to cancer. His already weakened body could not take the virulent drugs. His last months were spent in pain and he passed away on 5 February 2009.

No tribute to Veeraraghavan could be complete without a mention of V.R. Muraleedharan. They met as doctoral students at IIT. Two more diverse personalities cannot be imagined. What held them together remains a mystery to me. It was a deep bond, and Muralee stood by Veeraraghavan till fate conspired.

Muralee took the initiative to form The Dr Dilip Veeraraghavan Memorial Trust. Veeraraghavan's parents, the legal heirs, turned in all his savings and posthumous service benefits to this trust which provides scholarships to visually challenged and poor students. The trust also organizes annual lectures and music concerts in his memory.

PUBLISHED WORKS OF D. VEERARAGHAVAN

Books

Chennai Perunagara Thozhirchanga Varalaru. Translated into Tamil by S.S. Kannan and Puduvai Gnanam. Chennai: Alaigal Veliyeettagam, 2003. Originally written as a PhD dissertation titled 'The Rise and Growth of the Labour Movement in the City of Madras and its Environs, 1918–1939' (IIT Madras, 1987).

The Making of the Madras Working Class. New Delhi: LeftWord Books, 2013.

Articles

Co-authored with C. Ramachandran. 'Colonialism, Nationalism and Labour: A Study of Nationalist Politics and Labour Movement in the Madras Presidency, 1918–1922'. *Indo-British Review*, vol. XIII, no. 1 (January–June 1987).

'Genesis of the Modified Education Scheme of Madras State, 1953'. In

Rajaji 110th Birth Anniversary Celebrations Volume.

'Class Conflict and the Colonial State in Madras Presidency up to 1918'. *South Asia Bulletin*, vol. 10, no. 1 (1990).

Co-authored with V.R. Muraleedharan. 'Anti-Malarial Policy in the Madras Presidency: An Overview of the early decades of the twentieth century'. *Medical History*, vol. 32, no. 3 (1992).

Co-authored with C. Ramachandran. 'Congress, the Left and the Working Class: The Case of Madras Press Labour Union 1937–1939'. *Proceedings of the 54th annual conference of the Indian History Congress*, Mysore, December 25–27, 1994.

Co-authored with V.R. Muraleedharan. 'Disease, Death and Local Administration: Madras City in the Early 1900s'. *Radical Journal of Health*, vol. 1, no. 1 (New Series) (January 1995).

Book Reviews (of)

Tamil Revivalism in 1930s, by Eugene F. Irschick. *The Indian Economic and Social History Review (IESHR)*, vol. 25, no. 3 (1988).

Science and Empire: Essays in Indian Context, edited by Deepak Kumar. *IESHR*, vol. 30, no. 2 (1993).

South India in 1857: War of Independence, by V.D. Divekar. *IESHR*, vol. 32, no. 3 (1995).

PROLOGUE

THE CONTROVERSY IN CONTEXT

A.R. Venkatachalapathy

Nearly seventy years after its introduction in 1953, and its swift repeal a year later, it is difficult to believe that an educational scheme, drably called The Modified Scheme of Elementary Education (MSEE), could have had such far-reaching political consequences. The name that its detractors gave the scheme perhaps captures its import better: '*kula kalvi thittam*', 'casteist education scheme'. With the strident opposition that this scheme generated, its architect C. Rajagopalachari's (Rajaji) political career effectively ended. Following his exit, the process of de-Brahminization of the Congress party in Tamil Nadu accelerated and culminated in the rise of K. Kamaraj who transitioned from a 'kingmaker' in the province to later becoming the anointer of prime ministers.

The scheme and its fallout—the subject of this short book—makes for fascinating and insightful reading. To understand how it originated, unfolded, and was eventually given a decent burial one could do no better than follow the life and career of two major political figures of twentieth-century Tamil Nadu: C. Rajagopalachari (1878–1972) and K. Kamaraj (1903–1975). How a former Governor-General of India stooped to become the chief minister of a state, and how a backward-caste politician with little formal education dethroned him forms the crux of the story.

RAJAJI AND KAMARAJ

Since its inception, the Congress in Tamil Nadu had been dominated by Brahmins. Not incidentally, the very first resolution in the inaugural Congress session (Bombay, 1885) was moved by G. Subramania Iyer.

Brahmin leaders of the Congress had little popular appeal and were unable to mobilize the masses. The biggest challenge to the Congress in south India came in the form of the Non-Brahmin Manifesto (December 1916) which declared, '[I]n what passes for politics in Madras [Non-Brahmins] have not taken the part to which they are entitled.' This 'manifesto' was followed by the launch of a Non-Brahmin party, the South Indian Liberal Federation or the Justice Party, as it came to be known after its official English weekly. The ground rules of politics changed with Non-Brahmins staking a claim to political power. This political movement amalgamated with a cultural movement for Tamil identity and a radical social reform movement in the form of Periyar's Self-Respect Movement. The Congress was forced to cede ground to Non-Brahmins. As T.S. Chockalingam, the great nationalist journalist, observed in an insightful biography of Kamaraj, published in the wake of the controversy that is the subject of this book, by the mid-1930s it was clear that none but a Non-Brahmin could become the president of the Congress in Tamil Nadu.[1]

Three prominent Non-Brahmin Congress leaders emerged following the birth of the Justice Party: Periyar E.V. Ramasamy, Dr P. Varadarajulu Naidu and Thiru. Vi. Kalyanasundara Mudaliar (Thiru.Vi.Ka.). Rajaji was instrumental in roping the first two into the Congress. Ironically, it was these two who were to play a key role in the campaign against Rajaji (while Thiru.Vi.Ka. died at the height of the controversy). But even these three leaders remained uncomfortable in the Congress, leaving one after the other: Periyar in 1925, Varadarajulu Naidu in 1934 only to rejoin it in the last years of his life, and an already marginalized Thiru.Vi.Ka. in the mid-1940s. What none of these stalwarts could achieve was realized by Kamaraj: unchallenged leadership of the Congress, a long stint in the chief minister's chair, and a key role in national politics.

[1] T.S. Chockalingam, *Kamaraj* (1955; repr., Chennai: Sandhya, 2014), p. 58.

Born in 1878 in Thorapalli in the present-day district of Krishnagiri, Rajaji studied in Bangalore before acquiring a law degree.[2] Coming from an orthodox Vaishnavite Brahmin background, as a young man, he was witness to Swami Vivekananda's inspiring visit to Chennai in 1897. During the Swadeshi movement he was drawn to Tilak's politics, and attended the stormy Surat session where the Congress organization split. A successful lawyer based in Salem, he plunged into local politics, eventually becoming chairman of its municipal council in 1917. In the beginning of 1919 he moved to the city of Chennai just as nationalist politics was gaining steam under Gandhi's leadership. The 1920s saw his steady rise in both the provincial and national political arena. This paralleled his close relationship with Gandhi. Once described as Gandhi's conscience keeper (in 1933) and even

[2] This section on the parallel, and conflicting, lives of and the rivalry between Rajaji and Kamaraj draws from Rajmohan Gandhi, *Rajaji: A Life* (Penguin: New Delhi, 1997); T.S. Chockalingam, *Kamaraj*, and *1945 Tamilar Puratchi*, ed. Mylainathan (Chennai: Janayugam, 1957). I have also used V.K. Narasimhan, *Kamaraj: A Study*, rev. ed. (1967; New Delhi: National Book Trust, 2017) which often makes unacknowledged use of Chockalingam's Kamaraj biography. M.P. Sivagnanam (Ma.Po.Si., 1906–1995) provides an elaborate, pro-Rajaji, account of the rivalry in his autobiography, *Enathu Porattam* (Chennai: Inba Nilayam, 1972).

Chockalingam (1899–1966) was born in the same year as Kalki R. Krishnamurthy (1899–1954) with whom he often crossed swords. While Kalki was Rajaji's alter ego, Chockalingam was Kamaraj's great advocate. Coming from a distinguished family of nationalists, Chockalingam edited the pioneering 'quarter anna' journal, *Gandhi* (1931–34), and was a founding member of the literary journal *Manikodi* (1933–37). The first editor of the daily *Dinamani* (1933–43), he founded *Dinasari* (1944–52) after resigning from *Dinamani* along with the entire editorial team. He later edited a series of journals such as *Janayugam*, *Bharatam* and *Navasakthi*. Chockalingam's Kamaraj biography was written immediately after the education controversy, and was launched at the famous Avadi session of the Congress (January 1955). (On Nehru's demand, an English version was published within days.) *1945 Tamilar Puratchi*, published two years later, is a compilation of his combative editorials in *Dinasari* during 1945–47 on the clash between Rajaji and Kamaraj. As such, it provides a foil to Kalki's pro-Rajaji journalism.

heir apparent, Rajaji had to, however, yield space to Jawaharlal Nehru.

It was in the interregnum between the Civil Disobedience Movement (1930) and the first provincial elections (1937) that Kamaraj emerged as a major figure in Tamil Nadu politics.

Kamaraj was born exactly a quarter of a century after Rajaji, in 1903, in the trading town of Virudhupatti, present-day Virudhunagar. His hereditary community of Nadars had seen dramatic changes in its social standing since the mid-nineteenth century. Indebted to the British, they were staunchly loyalist and were key supporters of the Justice Party and Periyar's Self-Respect Movement well into the 1930s. The tide turned with the rise of Kamaraj.

A tall, lanky young man, Kamaraj was involved in the Vaikom Satyagraha in 1924. By the time of the Civil Disobedience Movement, he was in the forefront of Congress agitations, courting arrest on a number of occasions. He was also deeply involved in organizational work. At this time there were two major factions of the Tamil Nadu Congress, one under Rajaji and another led by S. Satyamurti. Kamaraj identified himself with the latter. When Satyamurti became the Tamil Nadu Congress Committee (TNCC) president in 1936, Kamaraj became the secretary.

From the time of the Non-Cooperation Movement Rajaji was a key man in Tamil Nadu's Congress organizational politics. Despite never being made Congress president, his all-India stature was never in question. In 1937, when the first elections were held under the Government of India Act of 1935 that gave provincial autonomy, the Congress won a sweeping victory under his leadership, trouncing the Justice Party. But the sidelining of his rival Satyamurti would have other repercussions as he groomed Kamaraj to challenge Rajaji.

Rajaji's two-year-three-month term in office as premier was eventful. He enforced prohibition in a few select districts, steered the temple entry bill in the legislature, and introduced sales tax. But when he introduced compulsory Hindi in schools there was a popular agitation against it under Periyar's leadership—as in 1954, Rajaji's headship of the government came unstuck with his intervention in education. As the British government drew India into the Second World War without consulting elected Congress provincial governments, it led to their resignation—it was, in fact, a godsend to a beleaguered Rajaji.

The war years further tested Rajaji. He supported the British war effort and opposed the Quit India Movement, contributing to his distance from Gandhi. In 1940, Kamaraj became Tamil Nadu Congress president by defeating Rajaji's nominee, and as no election was conducted due to the ongoing war and the Quit India movement, Kamaraj enjoyed a long term as president. The election had been closely fought, and the margin narrow: 103 to his opponent's 100. Writing in 1955, T.S. Chockalingam remarked that 'Tamilnadu's history was transformed by those three votes. . . . But for those three votes it is doubtful if he would be chief minister now'.[3]

The Rajaji formula which accommodated key elements of the Pakistan demand short of partition, so that India could progress towards independence swiftly, met with great opposition. Kamaraj issued a show cause notice forcing Rajaji's resignation from the Congress. While he put up a brave face emphasizing 'the value of discipline as well as the need for liberty of thought'—in the words of his biographer-grandson Rajmohan Gandhi—Rajaji had 'lost his Congress base'.[4] Rajaji's weakness translated into Kamaraj's consolidation of his hold over the party.

It was not until 1945 that Rajaji was rehabilitated, but not without controversy and bitterness. His attempt to re-enter the Congress was resented by the cadre which had seen jail life and police repression during the Quit India movement. While Rajmohan Gandhi states that he was readmitted into the Congress following his letter to the party president Abul Kalam Azad, in August 1945, it came about at great cost to the party organization. News came suddenly of Rajaji's election to the

[3] Chockalingam, *Kamaraj*, p. 64.

[4] Rajmohan Gandhi, *Rajaji*, pp. 238, 236.

TNCC from Tiruchengode (the small town where he had established and managed the Gandhi Ashram from the mid-1920s), an election of which not even the party president Kamaraj was aware. This further fuelled anti-Rajaji sentiment within the party. Kamaraj declared the election null and void. A TNCC meeting—the first after the Quit India movement and the War—was convened in Thiruparankundram (near Madurai) in October 1945. The Rajaji camp tried to mobilize support as the primary agenda of the meeting was to decide candidates for the approaching provincial elections. But, sensing the mood against him, Rajaji left for Courtallam without attending the meeting. Not only was the proposal to elect Rajaji as TNCC president defeated, but even his election from Tiruchengode was declared void. (This controversy was aptly captured by C.N. Annadurai in the phrase '*Kodu Uyarnthathu, Kundram Thazhnthathu*'—the rise of (Tiruchen) kode, and the fall of (Thiruparan)kundram. In Tamil, both '*kodu*' and '*kundram*' mean a mountain.[5] Adverting to Rajaji's defiance of Kamaraj's leadership, Annadurai was indicating that Brahmins had triumphed over Non-Brahmins.) The matter was brought to the notice of Azad who appointed Asaf Ali to enquire into it. Asaf Ali spent a week in Chennai eliciting views from both camps. In the event, even before he could submit his report, a compromise was worked out: the Tamil Nadu parliamentary board was constituted with three members from the Rajaji camp and five from Kamaraj's. Kamaraj was now the unrivalled leader of the Congress in Tamil Nadu while Rajaji had to remain content with his influence in the all-India party. A Rajaji admirer's remark that 'Kamaraj was a raging bull let loose' is not only reflective of the Rajaji camp's perspective but also captures the situation in the party.[6]

Soon another controversy erupted. In January 1946 Gandhi was to visit Chennai by a special train. Fearing surging crowds, the

[5] *Dravida Nadu*, 6 January 1946.

[6] Kovai A. Ayyamuthu, *Rajaji: En Thanthai* (Singarampalayam: printed by author, 1970).

train station where he was to de-board was kept secret. Rajaji failed to inform Kamaraj of this. (How Kamaraj managed to be present to receive Gandhi at Ambattur station is another story.) On his return, Gandhi, in a signed article in *Harijan*, stated that 'a clique' was opposed to Rajaji while he had the full backing of the party in Tamil Nadu. Stung by this, Kamaraj resigned from the election committee. His influence in the provincial organization was such that Kamaraj could defy even the Mahatma.

In the 1946 elections the Congress won 165 out of the 205 seats in the Madras province which then consisted largely of legislators from the Tamil- and Telugu-speaking regions. Despite Gandhi's opposition to T. Prakasam's candidature for premier, he won as the Andhra members voted solidly behind him. The divisions in the Tamil camp benefited Prakasam—the Rajaji faction abstained when it became clear that Rajaji could not win. In C. Subramaniam's view, Kamaraj 'was largely responsible for the election of Prakasam instead of Rajaji as premier'.[7] The Prakasam ministry survived for less than a year: 'As Prakasam ran the government more or less according to his own wishes, he rubbed many members on the wrong side besides Kamaraj.'[8] Prakasam was replaced by Omandur P. Ramaswamy Reddiar in March 1947. A man of little formal education, Ramaswamy Reddiar proved to be a fine administrator. Known for his honesty and integrity, he nonetheless proved to be unpopular with his fellow legislators. In two years' time he too was replaced—the relationship between Ramaswamy Reddiar and Kamaraj 'getting strained'.[9] Kamaraj's choice fell on P.S. Kumaraswamy Raja. Kamaraj's control of the party was such that, C. Subramaniam conceded, he 'came to be known as "the Kingmaker"'.[10]

[7] C. Subramaniam, *Hand of Destiny: Memoirs*, vol. 1, *The Turning Point* (Bombay: Bharatiya Vidya Bhavan, 1993), p. 79.

[8] Narasimhan, *Kamaraj*, pp. 42–3.

[9] Subramaniam, *Hand of Destiny*, vol. 1, p. 122.

[10] Ibid., p. 79.

Repeatedly defeated on his home turf, Rajaji now focused on national politics in the context of Independence. In 1947 he became the first governor of West Bengal. Soon he became the first—and last—Indian governor-general. Rajaji narrowly missed becoming India's first president, but he was subsequently inducted into Nehru's cabinet (as minister without portfolio). Given his differences with Nehru, especially after Vallabhbhai Patel's death, this too was not to last.

How Rajaji returned to the south, to once again continue the tussle with Kamaraj, forms the context of this book. To carry the story further we need to turn to the first general elections in independent India.

1952 ELECTIONS AND AFTER

Held in early 1952, India's first general elections were historic: the world's largest democracy went for elections on a universal adult franchise. In Tamil Nadu too it proved historic, for very different reasons. The party which had led India to independence failed to win a majority. The Congress managed to win only 152 of the 375 seats in the legislature. Even the chief minister (as the premier was now called, after India became a constitutional republic in 1950) Kumaraswamy Raja lost. Only two ministers survived. The Communist Party of India won over 60 seats, mostly from the Andhra region and from Malabar. Independents won another 60 odd seats. In Andhra, the Congress managed only 43 of 143 seats, and fared even worse in Malabar, with just 4 out of 29 seats. The bulk of Congress's seats had come from the Tamil region—96 of the 190 seats—but it was a huge blow to Kamaraj nevertheless. His status as kingmaker was now seriously in question.

It was in this situation that Rajaji made what was a most unlikely return to Tamil Nadu politics.

Despite losing his own seat, Prakasam had cobbled up a front—the United Democratic Front—that included the Communists, and staked a claim to form the government. This had to be thwarted if

Congress was to govern the state. Kumaraswamy Raja refused to continue by taking recourse to election to the legislative council, the upper house in the bicameral legislature.

When the first talk about Rajaji becoming chief minister circulated it was dismissed with disbelief. Rajaji's alter ego, the accomplished writer and journalist Kalki R. Krishnamurthy commented with characteristic wit: 'It's like inviting Ramana Maharishi to become a municipal commissioner.'[11] Well, the Maharishi might not have taken charge of a municipal council but the former Governor-General did become chief minister.

Contrary to what his admirers might have thought, Rajaji found the 'proposition . . . exciting—it had a scent of poetic justice'.[12] Apart from the fact that it was Prakasam who had pipped him for the position in 1946, there had been much bitterness between them even leading to a defamation suit. But more importantly, the same partymen who had rejected him then were now at his doorstep pleading with him to take up the reins. Kamaraj himself came to Rajaji's Bazullah Road home to persuade him. The logic ran on these lines: 'if with his prestige [Rajaji] formed a ministry, it would survive, most of the smaller parties and independents would support it'.[13]

However, the process was long. It took about two months after the slow trickling in of election results before Rajaji was sworn in on 10 April 1952. There were many reasons for the delay—Rajaji's obduracy

[11] *Kalki*, 30 March 1952, quoted in Sunda, *Ponniyin Puthalvar* (Chennai: Vanathi Pathippagam, 1976), p. 770. Kalki R. Krishnamurthy (1899–1954) began his journalistic career in the early 1920s in Thiru.Vi.Ka.'s *Navasakthi*. Rajaji's great admirer, he edited the Tamil temperance journal, *Vimochanam*, published from the Tiruchengode Gandhi Ashram. He made his name as *de facto* editor of S.S. Vasan's *Ananda Vikatan*. After quitting *Vikatan* in 1941 he launched his own journal, *Kalki*. A prolific writer, he won everlasting popularity with his widely-read historical romances. His journalism provides the most faithful—and passionate—articulation and justification of Rajaji's views on everything.

[12] Rajmohan Gandhi, *Rajaji*, p. 334.

[13] Ibid., p. 333.

in having his way not being the least of them. For a start, he refused—much against Nehru's advice—to face the electorate, preferring to be elected to the upper house. Once again, contrary to Nehru's view not to induct members who had contested against the Congress, he roped in Manickavelu Naicker, leader of the Commonweal Party, into the cabinet. In making the choice of a cabinet with fifteen ministers, Rajaji 'acted with finality' declaring that 'all appointments are closed'.[14] Calling on the support of all members, except the Communists, he easily won the confidence vote 200 to 151.

For a man who had expressed initial unwillingness to accept office due to ill health, Rajaji was characteristically busy during his term in office. Quick on his toes in the legislature, he took on the Opposition, especially the Communists, with great gusto. 'I am here to save my country from the traps and the dangers of the Communist party. . . . I am your enemy number one, and may I say you are my enemy number one.'[15]

In terms of administration, Rajaji did away with food control which had encouraged black marketeering and runaway prices. Nature favoured him with a good monsoon. As Veeraraghavan points out, a legislation that helped mitigate the misery of small and tenant farmers of Thanjavur was also passed. The Rajaji government did its best to alleviate the sufferings of handloom weavers. An administrator who had won praise even from his British masters and bureaucrats, Rajaji was in full form running an efficient administration, moving files, writing copious marginal notes, and keeping ICS officers busy. But trouble lurked round the corner. Its first sign appeared in the form of a Congress man fasting unto death demanding a separate Telugu-speaking state of Andhra.

[14] Ibid., p. 338.

[15] Quoted in ibid., p. 339.

ANDHRA STATE FORMATION

From the later nineteenth century, the gradual rise of Indian nationalist politics had been paralleled by the emergence of linguistic and regional consciousness across India.[16] The provinces of British India reflected the history of the East India Company's annexation of various kingdoms and their subsequent accommodation with paramount power. Consequently, the provinces showed little cultural or linguistic homogeneity. Madras Presidency was particularly straggling, incorporating regions in present-day Tamil Nadu, Andhra Pradesh, Telangana, Kerala, Karnataka, and even Odisha—it was more an ethnological museum than a cultural region or a viable administrative entity in a democratic nation.

Telugu-speaking people constituted the second largest section of the presidency, next only to the Tamils. '[T]he first signs of Andhra movement began to appear in 1909'.[17] Demands were raised for a separate province of Andhra for Telugu speakers.

Such demands, however, sat uneasily with nationalist sentiment. Subramania Bharati, the nationalist poet who himself wrote songs in praise of the Tamil cultural region, commented upon the Andhra Mahasabha's annual conference at Nellore (1917) and its demand for a separate province: acknowledging the genuineness of the resolutions, he, however, asserted that national unity was the need of the hour.[18] But the demands of regional sentiment and linguistic pride, the products of the very same processes that created the 'imagined community' of the nation, pressed on.

[16] This section is largely based on A.R. Venkatachalapathy, '"Madras Manade": How Chennai Remained the Capital of Tamil Nadu', in *Chennai, Not Madras: Perspectives on the City*, ed. Venkatachalapathy (Mumbai: Marg Foundation, 2006). The best account of the Andhra movement remains K.V. Narayana Rao, *The Emergence of Andhra Pradesh* (Bombay: Popular Prakashan, 1973).

[17] D.A. Washbrook, *The Emergence of Provincial Politics: The Madras Presidency, 1870–1920* (Cambridge: Cambridge University Press, 1976), p. 250.

[18] 'Telunga Mahasabhai', *Swadesamitran*, 9 June 1917.

By 1920, following its Nagpur session, the Congress had reorganized itself on linguistic lines. Separate committees came into existence for Tamil Nadu and Andhra. Meanwhile the demand for the formation of linguistic provinces continued. In 1938, with the first Congress ministry in government, the Madras Legislative Assembly passed resolutions 'to recommend to the Government of India to request the British Government to form separate Provinces for the Tamil, Telugu, Kannada, and Kerala regions in the Madras Province'.[19] The fall of the Prakasam ministry in early 1947, a result of Congress factional politics, culminated in animosity between Rajaji and Prakasam. This further fuelled the demand for a separate Andhra.[20]

In June 1948 the Constituent Assembly of India appointed a commission headed by S.K. Dhar to examine the formation of new provinces of Andhra, Karnataka, Kerala and Maharashtra. The Dhar Commission recommended reorganization not on 'linguistic consideration but rather upon administrative convenience', a view close to Jawaharlal Nehru's heart given the traumatic experience of the partition of India.

Subsequently, the Congress (Jaipur session, December 1948) appointed a Linguistic Provinces Committee with Nehru, Vallabhbhai Patel and Pattabhi Sitaramayya (known as the JVP committee after their first initials) as members. Its report, submitted in April 1949, more or less accepted the Dhar Commission's views by recommending the postponement of linguistic reorganization by a few years. But Andhra was an exception. 'In some ways', the JVP committee observed, 'the demand for an Andhra Province has a larger measure of consent behind it than other similar demands.' However, it added ominously: 'Yet there is controversy about certain areas as well as about the city of Madras.'[21]

[19] Tenneti Viswanatham, *Supplement to The Journey of My Life, 1937–1957: An Autobiography of Tanguturi Prakasam* (Hyderabad: Prakasam Institute of Development Studies, 1992), p. 80.

[20] Subramaniam, *Hand of Destiny*, vol. 1, p. 195.

[21] *Selected Works of Jawaharlal Nehru* (hereafter *SWJN*), ed. S. Gopal, 2nd ser.,

The thinking of the Congress leadership was clear from the beginning: 'If an Andhra Province is to be formed its protagonists will have to abandon their claim to the city of Madras.'[22] Pressure began to mount. On 16 November 1949 the Congress Working Committee, based on the JVP committee report, recommended the formation of a separate Andhra province excluding the city of Madras.

A Partition Committee was formed in November 1949 and the Madras government approved its report in January 1950, 'based on a large measure of agreement'. But this too was mired in controversy with Prakasam signing a note of dissent that the apparatus of the new province should reside in Madras city until a new capital was ready.[23]

In the ensuing months the movement for Andhra heated up. Apart from numerous public meetings, one Swami Sitaram even undertook a fast portending perhaps the subsequent historic fast of Potti Sriramulu. Given Nehru's views that 'Personally I am opposed to bringing in fasting as a method of finding a solution for political problems'[24] and his categorical statement in the Parliament that 'Government will . . . submit to facts and not fasts',[25] the fast was broken only with the intervention of Vinoba Bhave.

As the struggle for a separate Andhra State gained from strength to strength, the situation drove both the state and central governments to exasperation. By early 1952, Nehru solely blamed Prakasam for the stalemate.[26]

In was at this moment that the 1952 elections were held. The new chief minister Rajaji's well-advertised view was that the clamour for linguistic provinces was a 'tribal demand'. But he nevertheless supported an Andhra province without conceding the city of

vol. 10 (New Delhi: Jawaharlal Nehru Memorial Fund), p. 136.

22 Ibid.

23 Viswanatham, *Supplement to The Journey of My Life*, p. 207.

24 Nehru to P.S. Kumaraswamy Raja, chief minister of Madras, 15 August 1951, *SWJN*, 2nd ser., vol. 16, bk. 2, p. 437.

25 Ibid., p. 442.

26 *SWJN*, 2nd ser., vol. 17, pp. 415–6.

Chennai. It was believed that the creation of Andhra province would give him a reprieve from the relentless attack of the Communists, whose legislators mostly came from Andhra.

The continuing pressure drove Nehru to exasperation, who refused the demand for the appointment of another commission. A plebiscite was ruled out, as it would not throw up a clear result. By July 1952 Nehru made it ever clearer that 'there ha[d] been so much argument on this subject that no one can say anything new or worthwhile.'[27]

This, however, was to change with one as-yet-unknown Congress man's fast. In a letter to Rajaji, Nehru had observed that 'Some kind of fast is going on for the Andhra province . . . I am totally unmoved by this and I propose to ignore it completely.'[28] But it was not to be. Egged on by Prakasam and Bulusu Sambamurthy, Potti Sriramulu had begun his fast on 19 October 1952. Soon Nehru had to sit up to listen. 'I do not know how long we can just go on postponing it. If we are clear that sometime or other we shall have to face it, it does little good to go on postponing this and waiting for a more favourable opportunity. The probability is that conditions will deteriorate.'[29] Conditions deteriorated dramatically. Potti Sriramulu's death on 15 December, after 57 days of fasting, led to large-scale violence in the Andhra region. Despite Nehru's bold statement that 'we must not mix up various things because a riotous mob did something,'[30] a committee under K.N. Wanchoo, Chief Justice of Rajasthan High Court was appointed.

Wanchoo's report, submitted in early February 1953, unequivocally favoured the creation of the Andhra State but equally clearly recommended that Madras city be excluded. However, he indicated that until a new capital was built the Andhra government could be temporarily lodged in Chennai. Nehru was inclined to accept

[27] Ibid., vol. 19, p. 403.
[28] Nehru to Rajaji, 3 December 1952, ibid., vol. 20, p. 235.
[29] Nehru to Rajaji, 7 December 1952, Ibid., p. 238.
[30] Nehru, 'Situation following Sriramulu's death', statement in Parliament, Ibid., p. 253.

this recommendation but Rajaji stoutly opposed it on the grounds that the troubles would spread to other Tamil areas where a sizeable Telugu population lived. He even went to the extent of threatening to resign from the chief ministership. A convinced Nehru now agreed that this move would only result in 'unseemly agitation, acrimonious controversies and administrative conflicts'.[31]

The state of Andhra came into existence on 1 October 1953 with the coastal and ceded districts of Srikakulam, Visakhapatnam, Godavari, Krishna, Guntur, Kurnool, Bellary (now part of Karnataka), Anantapur, Cudappah, Nellore and Chittoor. The residual Madras State was left with all the Tamil districts (except Kanniyakumari, then part of Travancore), Malabar (now in Kerala) and South Kanara (now in Karnataka).

Given this background to how the new state of Andhra came into existence, Veeraraghavan's comment that Rajaji acted like a Tamil nationalist is not borne by evidence.[32] The only point on which Rajaji was stubborn was on the question of Madras city being the interim capital of Andhra.

Dr M.V. Krishna Rao, the education minister who had formally announced the new educational scheme, moved to Andhra and C. Subramaniam, the finance minister, assumed charge of the education portfolio as well. Though the education scheme was announced during his predecessor's term, it was Subramaniam who faced the brunt of the attack in the legislature. The Director of Public Instruction (DPI), Govindarajulu Naidu, briefly opted to join the Andhra service but returned swiftly to continue in office in Madras.

With the formation of Andhra, the Congress had a comfortable majority in the Madras legislature. Rajaji was no more indispensable.

[31] Nehru to President Rajendra Prasad, 15 February 1953, ibid., vol. 21, p. 254.

[32] Antony Copley writes that Rajaji made 'a remarkably stubborn effort to frustrate the emergence of an Andhra state', A.R.H. Copley, *The Political Career of C. Rajagopalachari* (Delhi: Macmillan, 1978), p. 272. This is not quite borne out by the available evidence. See also Rajmohan Gandhi, *Rajaji*, pp. 342–3.

The opposition to Rajaji and his scheme, inaugurated during the course of the Andhra agitation, gained a new edge.

EDUCATION

Education was on top of the agenda of the early nationalists. The three aspects of the Swadeshi movement's agenda in the early twentieth century were indigenous enterprise, boycott of foreign goods, and national education. As Veeraraghavan discusses in Chapter I, Gandhi had clear ideas on what constituted national education. In the context of the Government of India Act of 1935 and the provincial autonomy that it envisaged, the Wardha Scheme (The Zakir Husain Committee Report) provided a detailed blueprint for elementary education. Gandhi's scheme of Basic Education emerged from this scheme.

Basic Education had five key components: 'the actual participation of the child in the learning process; the choice of a craft as a purposeful, creative and socially productive activity; correlation between subjects and craft selected and the physical and social environment; dignity of manual labour; and mother tongue as medium of instruction.'[33] In its essence, as far as elementary education was concerned, it was a common core curriculum for all children up to fourteen, organized round a productive craft.

Rajaji's scheme was rooted in the Gandhian plan. Veeraraghavan has detailed the genesis of the scheme, how it was pushed from above without debate even within the party, the response to it, and how it was implicated in the politics of the times. Here I would only add, based on new sources, further information that strengthens Veeraraghavan's argument.

Before we turn to it, what was the state of primary education at the time of the new scheme's implementation?[34]

[33] B.D. Bhatt and J.C. Aggarwal (eds), *Educational Documents in India, 1813–1977* (New Delhi: Arya Book Depot, 1977), p. 43.

[34] The figures in the subsequent paragraphs are drawn from *Report on Public*

Primary education in Madras State was imparted in lower elementary schools (Standards I–V) and higher elementary schools (VI–VIII). All these elementary schools were open to girls and boys. The government had made a policy decision to open elementary schools in all villages with a population of 500 or more. In keeping with this, the government had provided 81.4 per cent of such population centres (as per the 1951 census) with at least one school. Before the creation of Andhra, the number of schools stood at 21,873 (higher elementary schools: 2,338; and lower elementary schools—single teacher: 1,921; and other than single teacher: 17,614). The following are the figures for students studying in these schools:

	1952–54	*1953–54*
Boys	1,764,105	1,905,204
Girls	987,610	1,127,286
Total	2,751,715	3,032,490

These three million students were taught by 91,569 teachers (63,115 men and 28,454 women) of whom 87,865 were trained teachers. The government's total direct expenditure on primary education was Rs 68,078,636.

Veeraraghavan has set out in detail how the scheme was initiated. Within months of Rajaji's assumption of office, the Education Minister, in the course of a legislative assembly debate, announced the government's intention of reorganizing elementary education with a shift system and the training of children in their parents' traditional occupation. But this went unnoticed at that time. Based on an interview with N.D. Sundaravadivelu (1912–1993), the then Deputy Director of Public Instruction (Elementary Education), Veeraraghavan states that Rajaji had asked the DPI, S. Govindarajulu Naidu to work out the details of the scheme.

Instruction in the Madras State for the Year 1953–54, pp. 11–17.

At about the same time that Veeraraghavan was interviewing him, Sundaravadivelu was serializing his memoirs in monthly instalments in *Sathyagangai*.[35] The memoirs provide a full account of how the scheme came to be announced. Given the silence in the records about how the scheme was worked out, let me draw on these memoirs to flesh out the details.

One day in late 1952, when he was on an official tour, Sundaravadivelu received a letter that left him dazed. It was a confidential letter from Govindarajulu Naidu, marked 'for immediate attention'. The DPI wanted him, on instruction from the Chief Minister, to draft a scheme wherein elementary school children in the rural areas were to spend half a day acquiring skills in their parents' occupation. Sundaravadivelu was in a dilemma: whether to carry out orders or to protest a scheme that, in his view, was disastrous to the children. He consulted a close benefactor who advised him that the job of the executive was to carry out policy decisions of an elected government; however, criticism of the policy, articulated in measured and inoffensive terms, could be made to the policymaker. Following this advice, Sundaravadivelu first consulted a senior superintendent in his office, one Krishnaswamy Iyengar, who pointed out that this was but an old scheme. In 1937 (as Veeraraghavan himself notes), Rajaji had proposed a similar scheme but the then DPI (R.M. Statham) had suggested giving it a trial before implementing it across the presidency. Krishnaswamy Iyengar fished out an old file, and the papers showed that the scheme had been experimented with in the Periyakulam *taluk* of Madurai district. As cautioned by the DPI, attendance fell rather than rose, and the experiment was dropped. When Sundaravadivelu

[35] The series commenced in April 1977, and the relevant parts of the memoirs would have been published at about the time that Veeraraghavan was working on this project. However, he seems to have not been aware of its publication. The memoirs were later published in three bulky volumes, *Ninaivu Alaigal* (Chennai: Vanathi Pathippagam, 1983, 1985, 1988). This section is based on volume 2, pp. 439–54. Distinctly lacking in style or literary flair, the self-serving memoirs are nevertheless detailed and chronological.

drew his attention to the shift system introduced when Omandur P. Ramaswamy Reddiar was premier and T.S. Avinashilingam Chettiar education minister, the Superintendent rightly pointed out that this was a measure meant for schools without adequate infrastructure and that it specifically overruled additional work for teachers.

Armed with this background research, Sundaravadivelu states that he wrote a long but carefully worded draft note, and passed it on to Govindarajulu Naidu, who endorsed it but stated that he would pass it on to Rajaji only if asked for his views. Many months passed, and there were no further developments. Sundaravadivelu was happy that, perhaps, the scheme had been dropped.

In late May 1953,[36] Govindarajulu Naidu, accompanied by Sundaravadivelu, set out to Fort St George. After a long meeting with Rajaji, when Sundaravadivelu waited outside the room, he stepped out and told him that a long evening of work awaited them. In the course of the meeting Rajaji had pointedly asked the DPI if he had reservations against the scheme, and helpfully suggested that, if that was the case, he would appoint a special officer for the purpose. When the DPI assured him of his support, Rajaji instructed him to draft a circular and send it to *The Hindu*, the *Indian Express* and other Tamil dailies that very evening. Even as the circular was being drafted by Govindarajulu Naidu and Sundaravadivelu there were calls from the newspaper offices. The draft completed, the circular was stencilled, cyclostyled and sent to the newspapers.

Early next morning the DPI received a call from the education secretary, K.M. Unnithan—incidentally, the two had studied together at Cambridge—who asked him sarcastically, 'From when did you become the government?' His reply that he was only carrying out the Chief Minister's orders silenced him. This was soon followed by a call from the Education Minister, M.V. Krishna Rao, who too expressed surprise that a policy decision of this magnitude had not been placed before the cabinet first.

[36] Sundaravadivelu is mistaken—this was in mid-April.

C. Subramaniam's assertion in his memoirs that Rajaji had conceived the idea in consultation with the Education Minister and the DPI is not borne out by evidence.[37] Veeraraghavan too is categorical that nobody in the cabinet or the secretariat knew anything about the scheme. Rajaji had also not taken his party into confidence—a matter that deeply agitated the legislators who were already disgruntled for various—justified and unjustified—reasons.

Rajaji was a compulsive note-writer on government files. Even draft orders did not escape his punctilious pen. As C. Subramaniam remarks, 'Rajaji particularly insisted that the orders issued by the various departments should be properly worded without any ambiguity. There was hardly any draft order that did not suffer drastic changes in his hands.'[38] But in the scores of government orders of the Education Department of that time there are hardly any jottings by Rajaji—we may take this as a confirmation of his opponents' contention that the scheme's genesis and elaboration were never discussed by Rajaji with anyone in the government. In fact, there is no government file on the actual genesis of the scheme—how it originated and how it was framed.

Rajaji made it his personal project. To critics, both within and outside his party, he had quipped, whom did Ramanuja and Sankara consult before making their pronouncements.[39] It was no doubt a brilliant rejoinder but not appropriate in a democracy.

An incident narrated by Sundaravadivelu demonstrates the personal investment Rajaji had made in the scheme, and how he was not averse to shrewdly using the caste card to win support.[40]

One day in August 1953, P. Sabanayagam, Rajaji's private secretary, dropped in at Sundaravadivelu's home unannounced—a most

[37] Subramaniam, *Hand of Destiny*, vol. 1, p. 205.

[38] Ibid., p. 180.

[39] Chockalingam, *Kamaraj*, p. 116.

[40] Sundaravadivelu, *Ninaivu Alaigal*, vol. 2, pp. 457–64. For another version, see Sundaravadivelu, *Ninaivil Nirpavargal* (Chennai: Vanathi Pathippagam, 1982), pp. 68–72.

unlikely act for an IAS officer, for Sundaravadivelu was a relatively junior officer. Sabanayagam produced a first class train ticket to Ambur on an express train to Bangalore. To a bewildered Sundaravadivelu, he explained that he was expected to speak at the North Arcot District Educational Conference—organized at the instance of Nathamuni Naidu, MLC—to be presided over by Rajaji. When Sundaravadivelu protested mildly that only an officer of the rank of a director or above could speak in the presence of the chief minister, Sabanayagam explained that his superior, the DPI, had been informed. When a cautious Sundaravadivelu telephoned the DPI, he too stated that he was equally intrigued by the impropriety but could hardly afford to disobey the Chief Minister. Sundaravadivelu travelled with Rajaji on the same train. At the public meeting, Rajaji called upon him to speak, indicating that he could take all the time he wanted to explain the logic behind the new scheme. Sundaravadivelu's speech made headlines in the next day's newspaper. A discerning reader can hardly miss the fact that he had been willingly misled, a fact Sundaravadivelu papers over three decades later when penning his reminiscences.[41]

Rajaji had displayed considerable ingenuity if not cunning in choosing Sundaravadivelu to lead the charge. Sundaravadivelu might have been a low-ranking official but he was a prominent member of the Non-Brahmin movement and a close relative (co-brother) of Kuthoosi Gurusamy, the prime lieutenant of Periyar and managing editor of *Viduthalai*, the Dravidar Kazhagam (DK) newspaper which was going hammer and tongs at Rajaji and his scheme.

41 Sundaravadivelu was rewarded for his efforts. Within months, Rajaji gave him additional charge of collegiate education. His rise within the bureaucratic ladder continued even after. In October 1954, soon after Kamaraj became chief minister, he was made the DPI when Govindarajulu Naidu moved to Tirupati to become the first vice-chancellor of Sri Venkateswara University. Despite having no teaching experience or possessing a research degree, using his influence in the Dravidian movement, Sundaravadivelu became the vice-chancellor of the University of Madras in 1969. In 1972, he got a second term, and was regretful that he was not given a third term in office!

Evidently, Rajaji staked everything in this effort. Apart from pulling the wool over Sundaravadivelu's eyes, he along with his ministers set off on a propaganda tour canvassing for the scheme, a matter that became a subject of debate in the legislature. One member wanted to know 'how many meetings were addressed by the chief minister and his cabinet members on the scheme and how much were the travelling expenses involved'. C. Subramaniam had to clarify that ministers were entitled to explain and defend the policies of the government during their official tours. 'While some meetings and conferences were convened specifically to explain the Modified Scheme of Elementary Education,' he confessed 'there were other meetings at which the Chief Minister, the Minister for Finance and Education and the other Ministers have touched upon the New scheme among other important subjects as it was their proper function and duty to do.' Naturally, the 'official tours are to be paid for from Government account'. When the member, in a supplementary, referred to Periyar's protest meetings, the question was disallowed resulting in a furore.[42]

THE DRAVIDIAN MOVEMENT AND MSEE

Veeraraghavan's treatment of Periyar and the Dravida Munnetra Kazhagam's opposition to the scheme, in my view, is inadequate. Even at the time of the Wardha Scheme, in 1937, Periyar had editorialized under the revealing title, 'Danger! Danger! Danger to Education!!!'[43] The editorial made a coherent argument about how Basic Education would reproduce the existing inequities in the education system. In a social structure where the educator and the educated belonged to different castes, the focus on craft would only perpetuate caste. Making an important distinction between '*arivu kalvi*' (knowledge education) and '*kaithozhil kalvi*' (knowledge of handicraft), Periyar argued

[42] G.O. No. 718, Education, 26 May 1954.

[43] *Kudi Arasu*, 21 November 1937.

that schools, rather than being knowledge imparting institutions, would not even resemble industrial training schools but be reduced to quasi-factories. He saw Rajaji's scheme as just another avatar of Basic Education, devised to harm the future of Non-Brahmin and other deprived sections of society. Given the time in which he wrote, and his ideological predilections, Veeraraghavan's uneasiness with Periyar's criticism is understandable.

Further, Veeraraghavan's comment that 'this agitation did not affect the masses much' might be somewhat off the mark. Periyar organized conferences, meetings, processions, and picketing across the state. Travelling brigades were constituted to carry out propaganda. Over 2,000 people were arrested, many injured with a few casualties, in the agitation.

As part of the *mummunai porattam* (three-pronged agitation[44]) of the Dravida Munnetra Kazhagam (DMK), the opposition to the scheme was a major factor in the rise to prominence of Dravidian ideology in the 1950s. In the 1957 elections, after this controversy, the DMK made an impressive electoral debut with 15 seats in the Assembly, becoming the primary Opposition party, and two in the Parliament. The DMK moved from strength to strength to finally sweep to power in 1967, ironically in alliance with Rajaji's Swatantra Party.

There was an interesting sidelight to the anti-Rajaji agitation. On 20 December 1953, at the peak of the agitation, on the beach across the Madras High Court, a massive public meeting had been organized to commemorate Milad-un-Nabi, the Prophet Muhammad's birthday. In a coup of sorts by the organizers, both Periyar and Rajaji were invited. Recovering from a high fever, Periyar made a special effort to be present before Rajaji arrived. The two men, who remained dear old friends despite their political differences, were meeting in person after

[44] The agitation was to protest against (1) the education scheme, (2) the naming of Kallakudi railway station after the Marwari businessman Dalmia as Dalmiapuram, and (3) Nehru's remarks that the DMK agitation was 'nonsense'.

At the height of the controversy, Periyar EVR and Rajaji share the dais at the Milad-un-Nabi celebrations on 20 December 1953.

years. The sight of the two sent the audience into raptures. Though both pointedly avoided any reference to the ongoing controversy, they emphasized the need for civil debate. While Rajaji stated that the fact of the two old friends seated together was a big statement in itself, Periyar remarked that even if the evening did not provide music to the ears it was definitely a feast for the eyes.

But by then the writing was on the wall. As Veeraraghavan elaborates, Rajaji found little support within his party. There was a mutiny in the ranks. The ruling party was at war with the government.[45] Rajaji was left to fight a rearguard action. His every effort to defend the scheme only fuelled further opposition. As has been pointed out, the merits of the scheme were like the mythical Harichandra's wife's wedding necklace—visible to no one except to Rajaji.[46] It was left to

[45] According to Chockalingam, the leading Congress members who were against the scheme were the veteran P. Varadarajulu Naidu, V.K. Ramaswamy Mudaliar, K.T. Kosalram, T.G. Krishnamurthy, Panchaksharam Chettiar and A.M. Sambandam. Chockalingam, *Kamaraj*, p. 119.

[46] Vasanthi Srinivasan, *Gandhi's Conscience Keeper: C. Rajagopalachari and*

Rajaji's ardent admirers and supporters to back him. M.P. Sivagnanam, writer and the leader of an independent faction called the Tamilarasu Kazhagam within the party, and arch rival of Kamaraj was one of the few who took it upon himself to defend him. In a propaganda meeting organized in Mayiladuthurai, he was attacked and suffered a bleeding wound on his temple. But even Sivagnanam, who backed Rajaji, pleaded with him to drop the scheme as it was putting the government on the chopping block. It was only diehard supporters such as Kalki who argued Rajaji's case unconditionally.[47]

When Rajaji resigned, he cited ill health rather than the politics that caused his resignation. Kalki's long editorial at the time of his resignation is revealing. Terming the two years of his reign as golden years, Kalki listed Rajaji's achievements, and blamed the ambitions of selfish MLAs for his resignation. No mention was made of the political processes that unseated him. Kamaraj's name is nowhere mentioned. And not a word was breathed about the education scheme.[48]

While Kamaraj was very much opposed to the education scheme, he was not in the forefront of the agitation. While Chockalingam states that the dissidents expressed their dissent through Kamaraj,[49] another sympathetic biographer notes, 'Kamaraj had been critical of the scheme . . . and had advised Rajaji to withdraw it. Although he did not direct the agitation against the scheme, he did nothing to restrain the critics, who came mainly from among the legislators from Tamil Nad.'[50]

Rajaji's political life did not end with his resignation—he remained a respected statesman. In 1959, he formed the Swatantra

Indian Politics (Ranikhet: Permanent Black, 2009), p. 64.

47 Kalki, *Amarar Kalkiyin Kalvi Chinthanaigal* (Chennai: Vanathi Pathippagam, 2008) compiles all the editorials and essays by Kalki defending the scheme.

48 'Irandu Pon Varudangal' [Two Golden Years], *Kalki*, 11 April 1954, reproduced in Kalki, *Vazhga Suthanthiram, Vazhga Nirantharam* (Chennai: Vanathi Pathippagam, 2001), pp. 527–35.

49 Chockalingam, *Kamaraj*, p. 114.

50 Narasimhan, *Kamaraj*, p. 52.

Kalki, 29 November 1953.

The Congress government is a boat which some Congress MLAs are trying to scuttle.

Party, and was the primary challenger of Nehruvian socialism. Kamaraj, as chief minister, led the party to victory in the 1957 and 1962 elections. Under his leadership, Tamil Nadu made solid progress in the fields of education and industry, laying the foundation for the state's development under Dravidian rule. In 1963, he gave up office under a plan that he framed (K Plan or Kamaraj Plan) wherein senior leaders were to resign from government office and work towards strengthening the party.

The next few years were halcyon days for Kamaraj. As the head of the 'syndicate' (group of regional Congress leaders), he was effectively the 'kingmaker', playing a key role in anointing Lal Bahadur Shastri (after Nehru's death in May 1964) and Indira Gandhi (on Shastri's death in January 1966) as prime ministers. However, Kamaraj's relinquishing of government position proved to be suicidal for the party in Tamil Nadu. In the 1967 Tamil Nadu assembly elections, the

Congress was trounced by the DMK alliance—Kamaraj himself was defeated in his pocket borough of Virudhunagar. Across India, the Congress lost in nine states and just about managed to retain power at the Centre. Over the next few years, Mrs Gandhi established herself as a leader in her own right, defeated the syndicate, and won undisputed command of the party.

In the 1971 elections, in a dramatic turnaround, Rajaji and Kamaraj—after the split engineered by Mrs Gandhi leaving behind a rump of an older generation of regional Congress leaders—came together to fight the DMK which was in alliance with Mrs Gandhi but lost comprehensively. Rajaji died the following year. A broken man, Kamaraj died on Gandhi Jayanti, 1975, some months after the Emergency was promulgated.

This then is the backdrop to the controversy. Based on an enviable command of the sources and a perspicacious understanding of the political and ideological currents in Tamil society, Veeraraghavan has provided a dramatic account of it.

But the book is also a product of its times. In my view, Veeraraghavan somewhat understates the power of ideology to create social change. Despite the analysis of educational ideas in the first chapter, he tends to emphasize political wrangling rather than the clash of ideas and alternative visions of society. However, as a young Marxist, Veeraraghavan was also convinced that until there was a complete transformation of society no change in education—rather, in any component of the 'superstructure'—could be effected. This tension is evident in the text. While being rather critical of the undemocratic manner in which the scheme was pushed through by Rajaji, Veeraraghavan seems to have had a lurking bias towards the virtues of manual labour. Perhaps this was derived from his reading of Rousseau, Spencer, and Dewey, already by this young age.

This study was written in the beginning in the 1980s, when the Communist parties were critical of the Dravidian movement. A consequent weakness of Veeraraghavan's thesis is his evaluation of the response of the DK and the DMK to Rajaji's scheme. He does not sufficiently appreciate the Non-Brahmin hesitance to valorize manual work when their aspiration was to escape its drudgery and graduate to intellectual labour. More importantly, the danger of reproducing the caste system and its ideology may have been missed.[51]

But perhaps this is too much to ask of a twenty-three-year-old student at the beginning of his academic career working in difficult circumstances. Veeraraghavan's meticulous marshalling of the data, and his understanding of the period is astonishing nearly four decades after its writing. Why he did not wish to publish it can perhaps only be explained as one more case of the best being the enemy of the good.

Whatever its merits or lack thereof, Rajaji's Modified Scheme of Elementary Education was sucked into times that determined the course of politics over most of the next half century. One could do no better than read Veeraraghavan's book to understand this politics.

[51] While no work covers Veeraraghavan's ground, there have been a few recent brief analyses of Rajaji's education scheme. See Vasanthi Srinivasan, *Gandhi's Conscience Keeper*, pp. 63–7; S. Anandhi, 'Education and Dravidian Common Sense', *Seminar*, no. 708 (August 2018), pp. 28–32.

Half a Day for Caste?

INTRODUCTION

This book attempts to study the Modified Scheme of Elementary Education introduced in 1953 in the Madras State by its chief minister, C. Rajagopalachari. The study locates the scheme and the reaction to it in the socio-economic and political history of the state and analyses its impact.

Described as '*Kula Kalvi Thittam*' ('caste-based education scheme') by its detractors, the scheme proposed half-a-day schooling for rural children with the other half of the day being devoted to training in the traditional craft of the parent; if the parent did not belong to an occupational class, then some other village craft was to be taught by the village artisan. The scheme ignited a stormy controversy. The specific socio-political environment prevailing in the state at that time added to the bitterness of the controversy, leading finally to the resignation of Rajaji from the chief ministership in March 1954, within nine months of its inauguration.

Many works have detailed the political career of Rajaji and other actors in this drama of the early 1950s. But their analysis is limited to the political aspect of the controversy. The educational aspect and the socio-economic philosophy underlying the scheme have been underplayed, if not totally ignored. The need for an interdisciplinary study with emphasis on the sociological and philosophical bases of educational policies has been felt, hence this modest attempt. The method adopted is the external-cum-problem-centred approach common in educational research. The external approach is adopted to analyse the socio-economic and political factors determining the development of education both quantitatively and qualitatively. The problem-centred approach analyses the educational problem sought to be solved through the scheme. This study demonstrates the limitations of an internal approach to the problem of education. This book also analyses the political crisis triggered by the scheme with regard to its long-term effects on political developments in the state.

The primary sources used for this study consist mainly of publications of the government, proceedings of the legislature, administration reports, gazette notifications, newspapers and journals of the period. Departmental files have also been utilized to the extent they were made available by the Tamil Nadu Archives; archival regulations that department files less than thirty years old cannot be perused prevented a verification of certain statements in regard to what went on between the Chief Minister and the Education Department before the scheme was launched. The Tamil Nadu Congress Committee files were also perused. Over a hundred books relating to the politics and social relations in Tamil Nadu, economic development of India with particular reference to rural economy, sociological aspects of education and the social, political and educational philosophies of Gandhi, Rajaji, Nehru as well as Western educationists have been used. Interviews with some important personalities connected with the education and politics of Tamil Nadu in the 1950s were also conducted.

The first chapter provides an overview of the movements for educational reforms in the West while pointing out their influence on the educational and political reformers in India. This is followed by an analysis of the diverse educational philosophies within the Indian national movement. It concludes with a brief description of the search for a solution to the problem of mass education in India.

In the second chapter, the preparations for the launching of the scheme, the details of the scheme as promulgated, and reactions of educationists, teachers, public figures and politicians are described. This is followed by a discussion of the transformation of the educational scheme into a political issue. The significance of the debates in the legislative assembly and the momentous resolution passed to stall the scheme are analysed.

The penultimate chapter opens with a critique of the legal quibbling over the resolution and passes on to a discussion of the report submitted by the Parulekar Committee appointed by the government in response to the criticism of the scheme. The drastic change in the political scene following the separation of Andhra State and the complete politicization of the controversy are then analysed and the factors leading to the exit of Rajaji discussed.

The last chapter discusses the educational aspects of the controversy following the submission of the Parulekar Committee's report. The reactions to the Parulekar Report, the stand of the Rajaji government, and the withdrawal of the scheme by the Kamaraj government are discussed. The second section, after describing the achievements of the Kamaraj government, asks whether the nation has really solved the problem of universalization of elementary education. The relevance of the Rajaji scheme to the future socio-economic development of the nation is examined in the light of the Nehruvian strategy of development adopted by the nation.

The concluding chapter draws out the lessons from the events of 1953–54, both in regard to the educational strategy for the nation and to the preservation of democratic traditions.

CHAPTER I

THE GENESIS OF THE SCHEME

Ever since the birth of the movement for the independence of India in the last quarter of the nineteenth century, nationalist leaders had been concerned both with the spread of education among the masses and about the quality, content and form of education which Indian children should receive. An intense search for a solution to the problem of mass illiteracy went hand in hand with an equally intense exploration of the right kind of education that could ensure the advancement of the Indian people, politically, economically and culturally. Nationalist educationists looked both inward to the heritage of the past going back to the Vedic Age, as well as outward to the progressive educational philosophies of the West going back to the dawn of the industrial revolution which sparked off a movement for democracy and freedom in a continent then rising against feudal oppression and clerical obscurantism.

The first section of this chapter surveys the movement for educational reforms in the West which influenced Indian educationists and national leaders, particularly Gandhi and Rajaji. This is followed by an analysis of the diverse philosophies of education in the national movement with Gandhi's Basic Education scheme emerging as the ruling educational philosophy. The last section describes the search for a solution to the problem of mass education in India. The position of the Rajaji Scheme in the two-pronged movement for mass education suited to the socio-economic needs of the Indian people is highlighted.

WESTERN EDUCATIONAL REFORM MOVEMENTS

All movements for educational reforms in the West had two aspects:

one concerning the universalization of education (the spread of education among the masses); the other concerning the content and the method of instruction in the schools (what is to be taught and how). In both these aspects, the movements were influenced by the concurrent movements of political and socio-economic changes in these countries.

Prior to the modern era, institutionalized education was the privilege of the clergy and the landed aristocracy. The rising commercial and industrial middle class fought not only to have the privilege extended to them but also to alter its form and content to suit the socio-economic and political structure and the material-technical base of the industrial society which they wanted to build on the ashes of the old feudal society. The old schools were intended to train religious leaders of Christianity while the education of the aristocracy was oriented to the mastery of the knowledge and norms of behaviour required in royal courts and diplomatic circles. The educational needs of the rising middle classes were different from the above: 'Vernacular' schools, where education was through the mother-tongue, sought to meet the need for training in writing and arithmetic essential to commerce. The commercial adventurer and the industrial entrepreneur needed the skills and knowledge of science.

Jean-Jacques Rousseau's *Emile* (1762), as influential and famous as his *The Social Contract*, was the harbinger of the new educational philosophy. Stressing the importance of physical activity and reasoning, Rousseau rejected the premature memorizing of words as harmful to the development of the quality of judgment: 'Reading is the scourge of infancy', he remarked. Hence, perception connected with motor activity and experimental investigation was fundamental. The story of Robinson Crusoe was to be the 'source book' for the practical and scientific problems which the child was to solve. Living close to nature and making all his own things, Crusoe represented the simplest industrial situation which a child should study. The study of industries, especially the division of labour and the exchange of commodities, was to be the approach to the study of social relations.[1] Rousseau did not favour institutionalized education. Emile's education was individual and personalized. *Emile* was devoted to the education of the individual in the then existing society; the true education offered to the new citizen of the social contract lies in participation in public life itself.[2]

Though inspired by Rousseau, Johann Heinrich Pestalozzi (1746–1827) of Switzerland tried to apply these principles to school education. Devastated by the Napoleonic Wars, the rehabilitation of the orphans turned vagrants posed a serious problem in early eighteenth-century Europe. Pestalozzi sought to reproduce in his schools the conditions of a well-ordered peasant's or artisan's home. 'The school ought really to stand in the closest connection with the life of the home, instead of, as now, in strong contradiction to it.' The school was useful to education only in so far as it developed the sentiments and the virtues which lent charm and value to family life. The factory system had not yet developed, and domestic industries and handicrafts predominated. Hence his emphasis on direct training in domestic industries, handicrafts and farming. In his *Leonard and Gertrude*, this ideal home is that of Gertrude where the children spend a large part of the time spinning under the direction of their mother, apart from receiving moral training. Domestic labour constituted the central activity of the home but it was supplemented by intellectual training, much of which was carried on while the children did the manual work.[3] Pestalozzian institutions established by Emanuel Fellenberg in Switzerland included craft training of the rich and the poor, with agriculture as the medium craft. 'School instruction occupied three hours in summer and four hours in winter; the remainder of the day being devoted to work in the field or garden.'[4]

1 Parker, *The History of Modern Elementary Education*, p. 181ff.

2 Colletti, *From Rousseau to Lenin*, p. 147.

3 Parker, *The History of Modern Elementary Education*, p. 311.

4 Ibid., pp. 316–7.

Friedrich Froebel (1782–1852) in Germany organized school training based on motor activity. Every child was to devote one or two hours to some serious activity in the production of some definite external piece of work. Froebel proposed to devote the forenoon to instruction in the current subjects of study, and the afternoon to work in the field, the garden, the forest, and in and around the house.[5]

The seeds of Gandhian educational philosophy were thus contained in the philosophies of education of the Western educational philosophers of the eighteenth century and early nineteenth century.

By the time Herbert Spencer (1820–1903) appeared on the scene, the Pestalozzian school practice had degenerated into formalism. Strongly criticizing the 'well-conceived but ill-conducted system of object lessons', Spencer put forward his own schemes of education based on his philosophy of extreme individualism, and an organic theory of society. Spencer was an advocate of 'laissez-faire' for whom the socio-economic system of his age was the culmination of the evolution of society. An uncompromising opponent of national education and state control in any form, education was a matter of individual concern. An individual process, education begins with concrete experiences of the child, calls for learning by personal discovery and approves itself as satisfactory by creating pleasurable excitement.[6] This Aristotle of Victorian Britain in its heyday of imperialist expansion was quoted *in extenso* by Rajaji while he was trying to sell his scheme to the teachers of Madras.[7]

In the United States of America, John Dewey (1859–1952) saw the importance of viewing the educative process against the background of social life. Schools should be integrated with society so that the students might later meet the challenge of gathering tension in the social structure.[8] 'Learning through work'—through activity related

[5] Ibid., p. 443.

[6] Ibid.

[7] 'Educational Reform in Madras State', *The South Indian Teacher*, June 1953.

[8] Ramanathan, *Education from Dewey to Gandhi*, p. 16.

to actual life, with adult occupation as the core around which the entire curriculum must be built—was his recipe. Dewey's America was at a stage of development far different from that of Gandhi's India. The industrial processes which the American child was to study and carry on in miniature were not the same as those of rural India which the Indian child had to study. Dewey's solution was for an increasingly corporate and integrated society in which a conception of individuality born during the period of competitive capitalism could no longer be retained.[9]

The kind of education that fulfilled the needs of the existing socio-economic system was not, however, always acceptable to the disadvantaged sections of the people. For example, W.E.B. Du Bois, the outstanding educationist of the American Black people, observed, 'There comes a distinct philosophy of education which makes the earning of a living the centre and norm of human training and which moreover dogmatically asserts that the subject matter and methods peculiar to technical schools are the best for all education. This doctrine is fundamentally false. . . . We must give to our youth a training designed above all to make them men of power, of thought, of trained and cultivated taste; men who know whither civilization is tending and what it means.'[10]

In the nineteenth century, the Chartists waged an incessant battle for an education different from that prescribed by the middle class for the 'benefit' of the working class.[11] Their movement for an independent education took many forms, such as corresponding societies, Owenite Halls of Science, and Chartist schools. It had its own educational philosophers like Lovett, the knowledge Chartist.

Their denunciation of the education then imparted to the working class was political.

[9] Wingo, *Philosophies of Education*, p. 189.

[10] Du Bois, *The Education of Black People*, 1973.

[11] Simon, *Studies in the History of Education, 1780–1870*, chaps IV–VII.

> Men had better be without education than be educated by their rulers; for their education is but the mere breaking in of the steer to the yoke; the mere discipline of a hunting dog, which, by dint of severity, is made to forego the strongest impulse of his nature and, instead of devouring his prey, to hasten with it to the feet of his master.[12]

The movement for the right to education was coupled with the movement for shorter working hours and the abolition of child labour. 'If the low wages and inadequate means of parents be such as to prevent them from educating their children, it is the duty of those parties who profit by their labour to provide the necessary education.'[13] Thus it was that the employers of child labour were compelled by law to release the children from work for a few hours and impart them education. The utopian socialist Robert Owen had already demonstrated the beneficial effect of combining education with productive work when he opened a school for the children apprenticed to him by the Poor Law authorities. Marx saw in this 'the germ of the education of the future, an education that will, in the case of every child over a given age, combine productive labour with instruction and gymnastics not only as one of the methods of adding to the efficiency of production, but as the only method of producing fully developed human beings.'[14]

Summing up this brief account of the Western educational reform movements, we may note that both the earlier battles of the middle class for the liberation of education from the clutches of the Church and the landed aristocracy, and the later battles of the working class in Britain under the Chartists, have features common to the national education movement in India, described in the next section. The

[12] *Mechanics Magazine*, no. 7 (October 1823); quoted in Simon, *Studies in the History of Education*, p. 230.

[13] Samuel Kyod in the *Labourer*, vol. II, 1847; quoted in Simon, *Studies in the History of Education*, p. 274.

[14] Marx, *Capital*, vol. I (1887; repr., New Delhi: LeftWord, 2010), p. 454.

educational philosophy of learning through work and the combination of productive work with education is reflected in Gandhi. Free public education or universal education is itself a product of industrial society. The meaning of the term 'school' is determined by the social context in which it exists and which determines its function.[15] Therefore, one's attitude to the school cannot be isolated from one's social philosophy and outlook. The movements for educational reform and the movements for socio-economic and political change are always interrelated.

EDUCATIONAL PHILOSOPHIES IN MODERN INDIA

Until the British conquest of India, the social order was based primarily on the village *panchayats* working on the basis of self-sufficiency. Agriculture and animal husbandry were the main vocations for the millions in the villages. The artisan industry was an important pillar of the economically autonomous village. Artisans were maintained at the expense of the whole village which employed their services to cater to their needs.[16] The village paid its tribute to the central government mainly in kind. Commerce with the urban centres was limited to the sale of the surplus agricultural product. The village economy was thus self-sufficient, subsistent, and stagnant. 'The structure of the economic elements of society remained untouched by the storm clouds of the political sky.'[17] Such a subsistence economy had little need for institutionalized education. Family apprenticeship was adequate for the reproduction of labour.

The British dealt a mortal blow to this village economy. The destruction of rural industry with the inflow of manufactured goods, the new revenue settlement which profoundly altered agrarian relations, the creation of a new landowning class with the insistence

[15] Wingo, *Philosophies of Education*, p. 297.

[16] Gopalakrishnan, *Development of Economic Ideas in India.*

[17] Marx, *Capital*, vol. I, p. 339.

on cash payment of a generally over-assessed revenue demand, the consequent change in the character of production from production for self-consumption to production for the external market, the conversion of India into a producer of raw materials for export to Britain and a market for British finished products, the encouragement of cultivation of cash crops, the construction of railways and the building of other infrastructure to serve imperial interests, the monopolization of trade by British traders leading to the liquidation of the old commercial class—all these caused the collapse of the traditional pre-capitalist self-sufficient village. Rural India was drawn out of a subsistence economy into the vortex of the international capitalist order with its attendant capitalization, commercialization and monetization of the economy.[18] The movement of the vast subcontinent under British political control and the radical alterations in the foundations of the economy necessitated the imposition of an administration system and a British judicial system built around private property as against the joint ownership that was prevalent before. A new class of government servants had to be created and groomed, a class, in the words of Macaulay, of 'interpreters between us and the millions whom we govern; a class of persons, Indian in blood and colour, but English in taste, in opinions, in morals and in intellect'.[19] Macaulay dealt the final blow to whatever native institutions of learning existed and planted modern English education instead, to train up a stratum of docile executants of the English cut off from every type of contact with their people.[20]

The dialectics of imperialist intervention and education yielded not only a class of civil servants but a class of entrepreneurs as well. The Indian national bourgeoisie was born. Indian-owned textile mills were started. The liberal professions attracted the most talented. The deep and abiding change in the colonial system brought into existence

[18] Desai, *Rural Sociology in India*, p. 788.

[19] Gopalakrishnan, *Development of Economic Ideas in India*, p. 31.

[20] Ibid.

a conscious political leadership. The new educated middle class found in the British bourgeoisie its obstacle to advancement. The national movement grew under the leadership of Dadabhai Naoroji, M.G. Ranade, G.K. Gokhale and Romesh Chandra Dutt, who believed in industrial development and a planned economy to ensure that such development served the needs of agriculture. This new educated middle class carried on work for social reform, for enlightenment, for education and modernization against all that was backward and obscurantist in India.[21] Ranade pleaded for vocational education. Gokhale agitated for universal elementary education. Until 1905, the national movement pinned its hope on the British government to initiate industrial and technical development and to usher in democracy. These hopes inevitably ended in frustration.

Given that the leaders of the national movement had no mass base, a social gulf separated them from the rest of the community. It was inevitable that a new leadership should arise with a new policy and programme. In Bal Gangadhar Tilak, the national movement found a leader who could transform it into a mass movement. Tilak and his associates came to understand that the weakness of the movement lay in the 'denationalized' and 'Westernizing' ideologies of the moderate Congress leaders. The British justified their political domination on grounds of the superiority of British culture over Hindu culture. The nationalists responded by upholding the ancient Aryan culture. The cults of Ganesh and Durga were actively developed. The right of an alien government to introduce social reform was questioned. They believed that a mass national movement of opposition to imperialism could be built by harking back to a golden age of Hinduism as the rallying point for the people. The climax of this phase of the national movement was reached when Bengal was partitioned in 1905.

Synchronizing with the agitation against the partition of Bengal, the National Education Movement was born: 'a system of education, literacy, scientific, technical, on National lines and under National

[21] Ibid., pp. 22–5.

control.'[22] Aurobindo Ghose wrote, 'Home Rule and National Education are two inseparable ideals; none who follows the one can fail the other.'[23] Tilak explained, '[W]here the people and the Government have different ideals of citizenship before them, there arises the necessity of National Education as distinguished from governmental education.'[24]

National schools and colleges were started in Bengal, the Punjab, Benares, Masulipatnam, Madras and Bombay. These institutions refused government aid and recognition. The National University was started in 1918 by Annie Besant with Rabindranath Tagore as chancellor. Though national schools and colleges aimed to instil in the students a pride in the glory that was India, they were equally concerned about technical and scientific education. Their objective was to produce patriotic scientists and engineers who would build the national 'Swadeshi' industry instead of clerks and lawyers.[25] The National Education Movement concentrated on secondary and higher education. As far as primary education was concerned, Annie Besant's conception was close to that of Madame Montessori.

The National Education Movement faded out after the inauguration of the Montagu–Chelmsford Reforms. Gandhi took over the leadership of the national movement in 1919, and gave a new turn to it with the launching of the *satyagraha* movement against the Rowlatt Act, followed by the first Non-Cooperation movement in 1921. A mass upsurge took place all over the country. The national

22 Resolution of the Calcutta Congress, 1906.

23 Quoted in Srinivasa Iyengar, *On Education and Educationists*, p. 198.

24 Ibid.

25 Ibid., pp. 205–6. According to Besant, National Education on the literary side gave primacy to Indian literature, history and philosophy, treating foreign writers, history and philosophy as secondary. On its scientific side, it included Western science but stressed Eastern science especially in medicine and psychology. On the technical side, it embraced all the provisions for the industrial life of the country, i.e. industrial chemistry, engineering, all crafts and agriculture.

movement reached the villages. When the Non-Cooperation Movement was withdrawn, the frustration that the withdrawal had caused was channelled into the constructive programme which Gandhi had formulated for keeping active the thousands of political workers who had joined the movement.

Thus, the socio-economic philosophy of Gandhi became the dominant philosophy within the national movement. Villages were to be regenerated by reviving the ancient village communities: each village would be 'a complete republic, independent of its neighbours for its vital wants'. The '*charkha*' was the symbol of economic independence as well as political emancipation. *Khadi* and village industries were to be promoted. Gandhi viewed the highly mechanized factory system as inconsistent with a non-violent society. Decentralization was an integral part of the social and productive organization of his ideals. Modern industry and technology which promoted consumerism were at the root of all tensions and frustrations, breeding greed and avarice. An industrial India would begin to exploit other nations. As for the exploiters, Gandhi preached trusteeship and class conciliation. The ancient India to which Gandhi liked the nation to return to would, however, be rid of such evils as untouchability, oppression of women, child marriage, etc. *Varnashrama dharma* would be preserved but without its evil of casteism and untouchability. An austere, self-sufficient, self-contented village economy was to be the goal of a free India.

The educational philosophy of Gandhi fitted in with his socio-economic philosophy. He rejected the deracinating system of education imparted in an alien tongue, producing a bureaucracy alienated from the people. He had conducted on his own many educational experiments in South Africa and, later, in Sevagram. These culminated in the Basic Education Scheme which Gandhi enunciated in 1937 in the pages of the *Harijan*. Like his self-sufficient village, Basic Education schools would be self-supporting—learning would be through a village craft, preferably spinning which was the main rural industry. Education would begin at the age of seven and last for seven years. It would be closely linked to local conditions. It would be full-time. A teacher trained in the philosophy and practice of Basic Education would teach the core subjects as well as the craft. The curriculum of the core subjects would be so devised that they were correlated to the craft in every aspect. Children coming out of Basic school would respect the dignity of labour and be self-confident citizens of the self-sufficient village community.

The Swedish Nobel-prize-winning economist and modernization theorist Gunnar Myrdal compared this effort to that of vocational education for the Blacks in the southern states of the USA (which, as we have noted earlier, the Black educationist Du Bois decried). He commented that, '[L]inking the process of education too closely to local environment and its traditional pursuits jeopardizes modernization which requires a kind of education that will prepare young people for mobility, for change, for integration into the large and even international community.'[26] Thus, Gandhi's educational philosophy ran counter to that of the modernization school which wanted India to become an industrialized nation.

The evolution of the socio-economic and educational philosophy of the modernization schools and the resolution of the conflict between the antagonistic philosophies are discussed in the concluding chapter. Suffice to say, for the present, the industrialists found it convenient to concede the arena of primary education to experimentation at the hands of Gandhi and his followers, while they concentrated on the reorientation of secondary and higher education to sub-serve the interests of commerce and industry. The conservation of the traditional pre-colonial society in rural areas was a concession to their rural allies in the common front against new forces challenging both.

[26] Myrdal, *Asian Drama*, vol. III, p. 174.

RAJAJI ON EDUCATION

Rajaji was a conservative who firmly believed in a Gandhian socio-economic philosophy. He too stressed the importance of the revival of village industry and cautioned against economic growth causing dislocation to the rural economy.[27] Though a reformer who championed the cause of the untouchables and women, he never sought to destroy the existing social framework or to replace it by a more egalitarian one. His views on *varnashrama dharma* were more conservative than even those of Gandhi. He believed in the continuance of the traditional family apprenticeship.

> Those threads of essential labour on which the nation's life depends have fortunately been kept unbroken by family tradition. Most children still assist in the work of their father and mother and learn the family trade without school or institute and learn it well. . . . The food is grown, the cloth is woven, the sheep are shorn, the cows are grazed, the shoes are stitched, the scavenging is done, the cartwheels and the ploughs are built and repaired, because, thank god, the respective castes are still there and the homes are homes as well as trade schools, and the parents are parents as well as masters to whom the unaspiring children are automatically apprenticed.[28]

However, unlike Gandhi, Rajaji did not believe in institutional education for children. Schools were prison houses, where they were imprisoning the pupils too long in the classrooms; he would be content if he could get the Madras teachers to agree only to that part of his scheme cutting down the school hours even if nothing else was possible.[29]

[27] Erdman, *The Swatantra Party and Indian Conservatism*, pp. 31–88.

[28] *Rajaji's Speeches*, vol. II, p. 13.

[29] *The South Indian Teacher*, June 1953. Rabindranath Tagore held similar

> Bookish education was harmful to the development of the child. In the years of childhood, it is the reaction to the external physical world that enables the child's talents to be evolved and to grow, and this is secured more by work and play than by a disproportionate concentration on the acquisition of the capacity to deal with symbols.[30]

Indeed, he would rather have no schooling at all. 'How can we reconcile our laudable aim of spreading education with the need for continuing traditional occupations and family apprenticeship?' Rajaji asked, and added, 'I am a moderate man, a man out for healthy appeasement of all kinds, and so I venture to suggest to the crusaders for compulsory primary education whether we cannot be content with three days in the week for schooling.'[31] Gandhi too considered it injurious to confine children to book learning but sought to solve the contradiction by correlating book learning to handicraft.

Rajaji differed with Gandhi over another aspect of Basic Education. Basic Education envisaged craft-trained teachers to teach children through a craft. Rajaji had nothing but contempt for such teachers. As early as in 1910, he had asked teachers to send the school boys during their leisure time to a potter or a wheelwright or a blacksmith.[32] R.M. Statham, the Director of Public Instruction (DPI), Madras, remarked in 1938 while noting the report of the committee drafting the new school syllabus, 'The proposal to utilize the services of local artisans for the purpose (of teaching craft) is in accordance with the suggestion by the Honourable Prime Minister on the subject

views and wanted to 'rescue the children from the grip of a mechanical system of education to call them away from the dead enclosure of classes into sympathetic relationship with nature and life.' Quoted by Srinivasa Iyengar, *On Education and Educationists*, p. 180.

30 *Rajaji's Speeches*, vol. II, p. 33.

31 Ibid., p. 34.

32 C. Rajagopalachari in *Proceedings of the Madras Legislative Council*, vol. V, 28 July 1953.

of curriculum of elementary schools.'[33] It was perhaps this conviction that made Rajaji opt for the Revised Syllabus in 1938 in preference to the Wardha Scheme of Basic Education.

Thus, as the premier of the Madras Presidency during 1937–39, he suggested to DPI Statham to implement half-day schooling with half-day family apprenticeship. Statham had reservations on its feasibility, as the experience of the Education Department was that attendance dropped on Saturdays when schools worked half a day. Besides, rural unemployment was high and there was a scarcity of artisans. Yet, it was introduced on an optional basis in Periyakulam *taluk* of Madurai district. The scheme was a non-starter as no child opted for it.[34]

Dr A. Lakshmipathi of Madras had written to Gandhi in 1937 making a reference to certain schools run by Christian missionaries where the schools worked only in the mornings, the evenings being spent in agricultural operations or in some handicraft work for which the students were paid some wages.[35] Rajaji was obviously impressed by this when he made the suggestion to the DPI. However, he could not see the implementation of his idea through as the government resigned in late 1939.

But the idea had so persisted in Rajaji's mind that when he returned to office as chief minister of Madras in 1952 he renewed his suggestion to the DPI to consider implementation of the scheme. The Education Department is said to have pointed out the failure of the 1938 Periyakulam experiment and adduced additional arguments against the scheme such as rural unemployment and the possible

33 R.C. 1493-E/34 dated 5 October 1938 of the Director of Public Instruction Madras. In this Rajaji anticipated Ivan Illich, a staunch crusader against institutional education, who said, 'Most teachers of arts and trades are less skilful, less inventive and less communicative than the best craftsmen and tradesmen.' Illich, *Deschooling Society*, p. 27.

34 N.D. Sundaravadivelu, interview, 19 February 1981. Sundaravadivelu, *Puratchiyalar Periyar*. [Also see Prologue for a brief account of the episode.—*Ed.*]

35 *Harijan*, 11 September 1937.

public reaction to discrimination against rural children. It is not known whether these objections were communicated to Rajaji or withheld by the DPI. Rajaji had his final say and the scheme was introduced in June 1953.[36]

Rajaji's Gandhian outlook, his abiding faith in Hindu *dharma* and *varnashrama dharma* in its pure form, his identification with the rural masses, his conservatism, his contempt for the school system, all culminated in the Modified Scheme of Elementary Education (MSEE).

UNIVERSALIZATION OF EDUCATION

Historically, family apprenticeship was the primary mode of transmission of technical knowledge and skill from one generation to another in the era of the self-sufficient, subsistent rural economy. This did not of course mean that there were no schools at all. According to William Adams, in mid-nineteenth-century India, there was a school for every four hundred of the population. There were two kinds of elementary schools: to one belonged schools proper, *patasalas* or *madrasas*, with a professional teacher who maintained themselves on fees and presents from the children; to the other belonged 'centres of domestic instruction' where either the father himself taught his children or a tutor was engaged to instruct the children of the rich.[37] Only the three 'R's (reading, writing and arithmetic) and religious ethics were taught. The age of admission was between four and six and the duration of study two to four years. Instruction was imparted at the residence of the teacher or the rich men who engaged the tutor. Only the male children of the well-to-do classes got the benefit of this rudimentary education.

Modern systematic school education commenced later. The Charter Act of 1813, reiterated later in 1833, enjoined on the East India Company to educate the people of India. There was, however,

[36] Sundaravadivelu, *Puratchiyalar Periyar*.

[37] Saiyidain et al., *Compulsory Education in India*.

little progress. Rather, the percentage of literacy in 1901 was lower than in 1822. The reasons for the poor performance were many.

Firstly, in the controversy over the kind of schools to be organized, whether the traditional oriental or the modern English, the Anglicists carried the day, with the famous minute of Macaulay and the sympathetic support of Governor-General Bentinck. This resulted in the neglect of indigenous schools, the only agency that could have spread mass education. The Education Department, created in 1855, virtually closed all indigenous schools in the name of efficiency. Modern primary schools were too few and too costly to deliver the goods.

Secondly, the emphasis was on higher education through the medium of English. Primary education and Indian languages were neglected. This orientation of the educational system to meet only the requirements of administration resulted in the promotion of secondary and higher education to the detriment of primary education.

Thirdly, the educational policy was based on the downward filtration theory which evolved between 1780 and 1833. A governing class was sought to be created by educating the sons of *rajas* and *nawabs*. This failed. Then upper-class children were chosen as the agents, which too failed. Finally, it was decided to educate whoever was willing to receive higher education, hoping that these English-educated would teach the lower rungs. This too failed as most of the educated men preferred government services and pursued their own interests.

More than the misconceived education policies, the socio-economic and political policies of the British worked to the detriment of primary education. Centralization and urbanization of the administration, with emphasis on the development of the central, provincial and district headquarters, led to the neglect of the villages. The ruination of village industry without adequate urban industrial development resulted in widespread poverty. Imperial financial policies resulted in inadequate financial resources. Consequently, education received less than one per cent of the total revenue.

The need for spreading elementary education was, however, emphasized in the Wood's Despatch of 1854 which laid down the principles of grants-in-aid. In 1882, a commission was appointed to look into the question. This commission did not recommend compulsory education since it felt that an alien government could not use force and that radical social measures were necessary to create an environment for universal education which, however, would be contrary to the policy of religious neutrality to which the British government was committed. In any case, it was financially impractical.

The founding of the Indian National Congress in 1885, the deep interest in mass education evinced by socially aware Indians educated abroad, social awareness created by the reform movements, all gave an impetus to the movement for universalization of elementary education. In 1909, the Gaekwad of Baroda made primary education compulsory in his state and dispelled the misconception that institutionalized education was alien to Indian conditions. In 1910, Gokhale moved a resolution in the Imperial Legislative Council demanding that a beginning be made in the direction of free and compulsory universal elementary education. The resolution was defeated but there was an unprecedented expansion of primary education in the decade that followed, mainly by voluntary agencies. The National Education Movement, though, as we have seen, concerned mainly with secondary and higher education, also inspired the spread of primary education.

In 1919 the Montagu–Chelmsford reforms introduced dyarchy in the provinces. The education portfolio was now entrusted to Indian ministers. A number of provinces enacted legislation for compulsory elementary education in selected towns and districts. Some progress was made until the Great Depression. The Indian National Congress at its Karachi Congress in 1931 committed itself to universal free compulsory education up to the age of 14 years. With the introduction of political autonomy under the Government of India Act, 1935 and with the Congress forming ministries in eight provinces after the 1937 provincial elections, the primary education expansion programmes received great attention. Gandhi came out with his Basic Education Scheme, which, by making primary schools self-supporting was expected to fulfil the dream of universal primary education. He wrote in July 1937: 'As a nation we are so backward in education that we cannot hope to fulfil our obligations to the nation in this respect in the given time during this generation, if the programme is to depend on money.'[38] The school was to sell to the state what the children produced while learning through a craft and pay the teacher's salary from out of the sale proceeds.

The financial constraint in the implementation of the policy of universal compulsory free elementary education had agitated the minds of great educationists ever since Gokhale's efforts were frustrated. In the 1930s, R.V. Parulekar[39]—who will figure prominently in the latter part of the book—made a detailed study of the problems of mass education, comparing the education policies of various nations in the world when they were at the same level of economic development as India. He argued for a reduction of curriculum, raising the minimum age of admission to seven, shorter hours of schooling, higher pupil–teacher ratio (60:1) by an alternate-day-working or by a shift system.[40]

[38] *Harijan*, 31 July 1937.

[39] Ramchandra Vithal Parulekar (1886–1962) was a legendary teacher and educational administrator of Bombay State. After a long career as teacher and school headmaster he was secretary of the Municipal Schools Committee of Bombay Corporation. He was also the first director (1948–56) of the Indian Institute of Education, Pune, apart from being the adviser and secretary of Bombay's education minister. He subscribed to Gandhi's famous argument that traditional Indian education was 'a beautiful tree' that had been uprooted by the British. Parulekar believed in universal mass education and proposed an immediate expansion in elementary education through the adoption of radical methods such as whittling down the number of subjects taught and by resort to part-time instruction.—*Ed.*

[40] Parulekar, 'Mass Education in India' (1934) and 'Literacy in India' (1939), in

J.P. Naik, another eminent educationist, sought to overcome the socio-economic deterrent to the spread of education (the indispensability of child labour in the rural family economy) by limiting the hours of schooling to three hours a day and releasing the child for participating in the family employment. He also suggested rescheduling of school vacations to coordinate with the seasonal demands for additional child labour in the agrarian economy.[41] Statham, the DPI, in 1938, had also thought of a similar schema, though on a voluntary basis.[42] Certain Christian missions had adopted part-time schooling for over three decades.[43] One C. Krishnamurthy, speaking on the resolution in the legislative council, stated that he had proposed a similar scheme in 1944 at a meeting of the Teachers' Guild at Trichy, recommending two-and-half-hour schooling.[44] Acharya Vinoba Bhave devised one-hour schooling to impart the three 'R's, with the rest of the day being spent on productive work by both the teacher and the taught. Vinoba's scheme was tried in Telangana.[45] Thus, minds, great and small, had exercised themselves over the problem of socio-economic deterrents and financial constraints for over two decades.

The Post-War Reconstruction Committee for Educational Development, in its report known as the Sargent Scheme, had accepted Basic Education as the model for primary education. It estimated that it would take forty years to achieve universal free elementary education in India and that it would cost Rs 6.90 per annum per capita of population at 1938 price levels.[46]

Shri R.V. Parulekar Felicitation Volume.

41 Saiyidain et al., *Compulsory Education in India.*

42 Santhanakrishna Naidu, 'The Need for the New Scheme', *Madras Information*, September 1953. The author has probably attributed to Statham what was really Rajaji's suggestion.

43 Ibid. Also referred to in Dr A. Lakshmipathy's letter in *Harijan*, 11 September 1937.

44 *Madras Legislative Council Debates*, vol. V, July 1953, p. 503.

45 *The Hindu*, 13 February 1954.

46 Saiyidain et al., *Compulsory Education in India*. R. Suryanarayana Rao pointed out that the Retrenchment and Reorganisation Commission

The Constitution of India (Article 45) stipulated as a directive principle that the State should endeavour to provide, within a period of ten years from the commencement of the Constitution, free and compulsory education for all children until the age of fourteen. Had it been possible to implement the directive principle of the Constitution, universal free compulsory education should have been achieved by 1960!

A reference has already been made to Rajaji's views on compulsory education, expressed in his speech at Bharatiya Vidya Bhavan, Bombay, in 1949.[47] He had then opted, of course reluctantly, for three-day schooling. He rejected the shift system of 'cutting up of the day into two halves'. In his opinion, the school as well as the family occupation should have the benefit of mornings as well as afternoons. 'The farmer boys and girls ought to go to school on three full days and get the benefit of it, and be with the parents and cattle in the field or in the family workshop during four full days. We should not take away the morning and afternoon conditions altogether from either school or family.'[48]

When Rajaji assumed office in 1952, the state was still a long way from achieving universal elementary education. The enrolment was only 42.1 per cent of the children of primary school-going age.[49]

The financial constraints were serious. India was just recovering from the effects of Partition. Nearly half of the revenue had to be spent on defence. It had launched an ambitious development plan which required a large capital outlay. It was in no better position than the Indian farmer who preferred his child to labour and earn rather than learn. Education was starved of funds.[50]

---

had worked out the cost of universal compulsory primary education at 5.39/4.13/3.37 crore rupees depending on the time required for achieving the target (10/15/20 years). *The South Indian Teacher*, June 1953, p. 248.

47 *Rajaji's Speeches*, vol. II.

48 Ibid.

49 *Report of the Committee on Elementary Education in Madras State* (Parulekar Committee), 1953, chap. I, p. 4.

50 According to Adam Curle, educational strategy for development in

The hopes placed on the Basic Education Scheme as a solution for the financial constraints were belied. Basic schools, far from being self-supporting, proved to be expensive. The Madras government had come to a decision in 1952 not to expand Basic Education further. An educationist was constrained to remark in exasperation, 'I do not grudge the *jilebi* of Basic Education to be tasted by children in select schools. I pray that all children of the land be provided with the *conjee* of universal education for at least five standards.'[51]

Basic Education having failed to deliver the goods the only way to expand elementary education without incurring any additional expenditure on school buildings and teachers would have been to adopt the Parulekar–Naik formula of three-hour schooling and two-shifts working with the same set of teachers. The shift system was already in vogue in Madras State since 1949 when Omandur P. Ramaswamy Reddiar introduced it as an emergency measure to relieve overcrowding in schools. The 'OPR' shift system was intended as a temporary arrangement until additional buildings came up. The pupil–teacher ratio remained unaltered, each four-hour shift being served by a separate set of teachers. No out-of-school-hour activity for the children was contemplated. The sole objective was to defer capital expenditure.[52]

developing countries would require giving primacy to secondary and higher education. Curle, *Educational Strategy for Developing Societies*.

[51] Srinivasa Iyengar, *On Education and Educationists*.

[52] Sundaravadivelu, interview, 19 February 1981. The Parulekar Report said that the four-hour day was reduced to three hours in 1951 with the same teachers for both the shifts.

CHAPTER II

LAUNCH, IMPLEMENTATION, AND REACTION

PREPARATION

On 10 April 1952 Rajaji was sworn in as the chief minister of Madras State in an unprecedented manner. The Congress did not command a majority in the new legislative assembly. Rajaji had to employ all his political skills to outwit the Opposition led by T. Prakasam and supported by the Communists, the largest Opposition group.

It speaks to his attachment to his educational philosophy that one of his first acts was to examine the feasibility of implementing the scheme proposed by him earlier in 1937–39 when he was the premier of Madras Presidency.

Dr M.V. Krishna Rao, the education minister, announced in the legislative assembly in July 1952 that the government was considering the reorganization of primary schools so that some of the defects in the existing system could be eliminated. He further stated that it was also exploring the feasibility of arranging the classes in two shifts of half a day each, leaving half a day free for the child to engage in the occupation of its parents or setting its hand to learn some work on the farm or in the garden or the small workshop attached to the school. Provision of nutritious food to the pupils was also a matter that was being considered by the government.[1] Considering the storm that it later raised, this announcement made in the course of a reply to a Budget debate made no impact.

[1] *Madras Legislative Council Debates*, vol. III, 19 July 1952, p. 644. A reference to the proposal was again made by the Minister in March 1953 during the Budget session. That also went unnoticed.

Rajaji asked the Education Department to examine this proposal and work out a scheme. The Department was not enthusiastic and had objections to the proposal. But these objections were not transmitted to Rajaji by the Director of Public Instruction (DPI)—S. Govindarajulu Naidu[2]—who sat on the note until almost the end of the academic year.

Having waited long enough for the DPI to respond formally, Rajaji told the DPI of his intention to go ahead with the scheme. If he had any misgivings about the scheme, Rajaji said, he would appoint a special officer.[3]

Ultimately, the DPI fell in line with Rajaji. On 16 April 1953 he issued a circular to all district educational officers instructing them to prepare for the implementation of the scheme in the academic year commencing in June 1953. Until this point, nobody in the cabinet or the secretariat except Rajaji knew about the scheme.[4]

THE SCHEME LAUNCHED

The details of the scheme were as below.[5]

[2] Govindarajulu Naidu was a barrister and also had a law degree from Cambridge. Before being appointed as DPI, he was a professor at the Madras Law College. C. Subramaniam, education minister for most of the time period covered in this book, had been his student there.—*Ed.*

[3] Sundaravadivelu, interview, 19 February 1981. [C. Subramaniam recalls in his memoirs that Rajaji had conceived the idea in consultation with the Education Minister and the DPI. This is not borne out by available evidence.—*Ed.*]

[4] Sundaravadivelu, ibid. The charge that even the Education Minister was not aware of the issue of the circular was made by S. Ramakrishnaiah, an MLC (*Madras Legislative Council Debates*, vol. V, p. 468).

[5] *The Hindu*, 17 and 18 April 1953; *Madras Information*, June 1953, p. 10.

['Note on Modified Scheme' in G.O. No. 1872, Education, 4 August 1953, provides a more elaborate description of the scheme. While the substance is the same a few additional points missing here may be noted. 'In the case of girls it is expected that generally they will find enough activities in their homes. But parents who wish their girls to learn any craft or other work

The scheme was to be applicable only to non-Basic elementary schools in rural areas. Basic schools and primary schools in urban areas are not covered by the scheme.

1. The school day of the pupil in the primary school would be reduced to 3 hours a day. The working week was to be extended to six days if necessary.
2. Every school would be divided into two batches; one batch to work for three hours in the morning and the other for three hours in the afternoon.
3. The same teachers were to handle both batches.
4. The pupils would have work in school for 20 to 24 periods per week as against 35 periods earlier.
5. There would be no lowering of standards in language, elementary mathematics, history and geography, hygiene, civics and moral instruction. The same number of periods were to be allotted for each of these subjects and the same syllabus was to be followed.
6. The other half of the day when the pupils were not at school was to be spent by the pupils helping their parents in their occupation if they belonged to occupational classes.
7. The pupils who did not belong to families of occupational classes were to be attached to a farmer or a craftsman in the village for learning a trade. Such pupils would work like apprentices under a craftsman. There was to be no supervision by any school teacher. The craftsman would be the craft

---

in the villages along with boys separately may be allowed the opportunity.' Further 'during the agricultural seasons many of the elder children may be encouraged to observe, and even participate, in the various lighter agricultural operations going on in and around the village; it will be in the other seasons that the need will largely arise for promoting a programme of other activities for all children.' Success was to be judged by how 'happy and usefully engaged' the children were outside class hours. There was to be no rigidity in activities during their time outside.—*Ed.*]

teacher and was required to maintain an attendance register indicating that the boys were present during the allotted time.

8. Provision was to be made for teaching more than one craft suitable to the locality. Arrangements were to be made with the farmers in the village and pupils attached to each farmer so that they could learn the methods of cultivation.
9. Pupils were to be organized to render social services to the village in all possible ways.
10. When there were no local craftsmen it was necessary to encourage one to come and settle in the village in the vicinity of the school. Since he would require a place to serve as his work spot a craft shed was to be erected within the premises of the school if the school had a large compound.
11. It was estimated that such special arrangements for craft education may be required by not more than five to ten pupils from non-occupational classes.
12. A village school council consisting of willing and capable persons was to be constituted in each village to help arrange craft training.
13. The scheme was to come into effect during the school year of 1953–54 (commencing June 1953).

A conference of headmasters of Madras city schools was held on 23 April 1953 when the DPI explained the salient features of the scheme.[6] The objectives of the scheme were stated in terms of educational philosophy. There was no attempt to justify it on financial grounds. Nor was it a measure aimed at universalization of education. The existing system of education led to the growth of a new class of educated people, a new caste constituting a small minority and secluded from the rest of the population; it incapacitated them from physical work, and developed in them a craze for white-collar jobs, which unfortunately were not available in sufficient numbers.

[6] *The Hindu*, 24 April 1953.

Incapable of doing manual work, the educated unemployed felt helpless. Further, the student was alienated from his family and village environment. The burden of long school hours impaired the health of young school children, and deprived them of opportunities to engage themselves in village activities that would improve their general knowledge and make them useful to the community. The Modified Scheme of Elementary Education (MSEE), it was argued, would not only remove these evils, but was also educationally sound.

REACTION TO THE SCHEME

Once the scheme was formally announced, it evoked strong reactions from diverse sections of society. Teachers, educationists and politicians of all shades including a section of Congress men voiced their protest against the scheme. Each had their own sectional interests or philosophy for raising their objections. The protest was not only against the contents of the scheme, but also the very manner in which it was being introduced.

Opposition to the Manner of Introduction

Rajaji had claimed that the scheme would revolutionize the education system. It was therefore asked why such a radical reform was not placed before the public for discussion, before taking the decision to introduce it. The South India Teachers' Union (SITU) at its annual convention held at Mangalore in May 1953 expressed its displeasure at the way the scheme was sought to be imposed without proper deliberation and requested the government to refer the scheme to an expert committee.[7]

[7] *The South Indian Teacher*, May 1953, p. 218. [The resolutions passed at this convention came in for particularly hard criticism from Kalki, who observed that the fact that teachers opposed this scheme caused no surprise; it would be cause for surprise only if they had welcomed it. *Kalki*, 24 June 1953, in Kalki, *Amarar Kalkiyin Kalvi Chinthanaigal* (Chennai: Vanathi Pathippagam, 2008), pp. 164–5. Kalki further ridiculed them as being 'crazy

The entire Opposition in the legislative assembly unequivocally condemned the manner in which the scheme was being hustled through, without taking the legislature into confidence. The house should have been consulted before the government took a decision on such a vital matter affecting the future of the nation. It was argued that it was highly anti-democratic to present the house with a fait accompli.[8] Adjournment motions were tabled drawing the attention of the government to the apprehension of parents, teachers and other sections of the people.[9] M.V. Krishna Rao's defence that he had already hinted at the changes in his speeches during the Budget debates in July 1952 and March 1953 and non-opposition to his then statements meant acceptance was contradicted by Rajaji's statement that he had earlier introduced measures like prohibition and temple entry without consulting the house.[10] Rajaji was forced to admit that he had committed a tactical blunder in bypassing the legislature.[11]

Rajaji had always exhibited such supreme confidence in his own wisdom and intellect that he did not even for a moment think it worth consulting stakeholders. J.B. Kripalani's remarks on the introduction of Basic Education are relevant here:

> [I]t is not so much the matter as the manner of introduction of his schemes that creates misunderstanding and opposition. This

about bookish learning'. *Kalki*, 7 June 1953, in ibid., p. 173.—*Ed.*]

[8] Speeches of K.B. Menon (pp. 1701–4), Tenneti Viswanatham (pp. 1712–24), S.C.C. Anthony Pillai (pp. 1705–7), T. Nagi Reddy (pp. 1723–24; 1749), M. Kalyanasundaram (pp. 1725–29; 1743–44; 1747), P. Jeevanandam (pp. 1699–1701) and others, *Madras Legislative Assembly Debates*, vol. IX, 29 July 1953; V.S. Ramakrishnaiah (p. 463) and S.H. Parameswaran (p. 510), *Madras Legislative Council Debates*, 1953, vol. V.

[9] Proceedings of 15 July; adjournment motion moved by P. Ramamurthi, *Madras Legislative Assembly Debates*, vol. IX, July 1953, pp. 145–7.

[10] Ibid., p. 1686. Speech of M.V. Krishna Rao on 29 July 1953. Also, Rajaji's statement, *The South Indian Teacher*, June 1953.

[11] Rajaji's speech, *Madras Legislative Assembly Debates*, vol. IX, 29 July 1953, p. 1732.

> process of ushering in before the public the finished product of one's own labours may be appropriate in art, it is scarcely suited for introducing practical reforms in which merely passive acquiescence is not sufficient but active cooperation and participation are of the essence.[12]

CRITICISM OF THE SCHEME

Teachers

Teachers, particularly elementary school teachers, were the first to react adversely. The new scheme increased their workload by 20 per cent without any compensation. Qualitatively also, their work was made worse. They were turned into teaching machines, repeating the same lessons twice a day. There was no variety in their teaching work, no alteration of work and activity which had been a feature of elementary education. They were denied even the pleasure of watching their pupils at play or craft work.[13] More than the quantitative and qualitative worsening of their conditions of work, they faced retrenchment on a large scale as the pupil–teacher ratio now stood doubled. S. Natarajan, president of the SITU was one of the first to voice this fear.[14] The Malabar Elementary School Teachers' Union also passed a resolution to this effect on the very day the scheme was introduced.[15]

[12] J.B. Kripalani, *The Latest Fad, Basic Education.*

[13] Srinivasa Iyengar, *On Education and Educationists*, p. 139. Also, M. Krishnan in *Swatantra*, 15 August 1953. The South Kanara District Teachers' Guild complained that under the double shift system teachers were not able to find time to go to the nearest town for purchases except on Sundays when shops were closed (*The South Indian Teacher*, July 1953).

[14] *The Hindu*, 14 May 1953. [Kalki termed this a baseless fear. From *Kalki*, 24 May 1953, reproduced in Kalki, *Amarar Kalkiyin Kalvi Chinthanaigal*, pp. 165–6.—*Ed.*]

S. Ramakrishnaiah characterized the scheme as 'Retrenchment Scheme of Elementary Education'. *Madras Legislative Council Debates*, vol. V, p. 465.

[15] Resolution quoted by T.C. Narayana Nambiar, *Madras Legislative Assembly*

Though the circular introducing the scheme had not specified any revised pupil–teacher ratio, a doubling was implied. It was only after the report of the Parulekar Committee was released that the Education Department issued a circular in February 1954 revising the pupil–teacher ratio as below:

> Local Boards: from 35:1 (1953) to 60:1 from June 1954, both sessions taken together.
>
> Aided Schools: From 30:1 (1953) to 40:1 (1955) and 50:1 (1956).
>
> Teachers rendered surplus would be utilized for opening new schools or for teaching higher age groups.[16]

The government tried to allay the fears of retrenchment by assuring that no teacher would lose his job. Yet, the apprehension persisted and was real to an extent as certain local bodies and private managements started to retrench surplus teachers.

T.C. Narayana Nambiar, MLA from Malabar pointed out that in Malabar, even if all the children of schoolgoing age were enrolled, nearly thirty per cent of teachers would be surplus if the new pupil–teacher ratio were adopted.[17] The teachers were not, therefore, satisfied with the assurances and showed hostility to the scheme.

Educationists

Advocates of Basic Education and conventional schooling alike opposed the scheme.

Supporters of Basic Education had always opposed the shift system or adoption of shorter working hours at the primary level. They wanted the children to be at school the whole day, receiving education through craft under the supervision of the trained teacher.

Debates, vol. XII.

16 *The Hindu*, 3 February 1954.

17 *Madras Legislative Assembly Debates*, vol. XIII, March 1954, p. 1164.

J.C. Kumarappa, the renowned Gandhian economist and educationist, considered the scheme a deviation rather than a derivation from Basic Education. According to him, Basic Education and the modified education scheme were irreconcilably different.[18]

Firstly, in Basic Education the teacher's responsibility for the development of the personality and character of the child, his hygiene habits and training was fixed high; the teacher had to impart learning, inculcate craft, and integrate learning and craft. He could find joy in his work as he participated in the work of the children. In Rajaji's scheme, the teacher was reduced to a teaching machine, playing no part in the inculcation of craft or in the play activities of the child.[19]

Secondly, in Basic Education, literacy was correlated to craft training. Education and craft were to go hand in hand and were to be taught within the school by the teacher. In Rajaji's scheme, it was education at school and craft at home, with no attempt at correlating the two.[20] An educationist commented wryly: 'Would it not be complete Basic Education if the children do not attend school at all as everything can be learnt realistically in a normal setting?'[21]

Despite the fundamental difference between the two schemes, two advocates of Basic Education, Dr Zakir Husain and G. Ramachandran, extended their support to the scheme. The two men considered it a transitional arrangement until the resources improved and the ultimate goal of Basic Education became feasible. G. Ramachandran, the Gandhian educationist and co-founder of Gandhigram Rural Institute, was appointed educational advisor to the government to look after the implementation of the scheme.[22]

Liberal educationists believed the scheme violated all the principles of education. They did not accept Rajaji's view that schools

18 *The Hindu*, 17 July 1953.

19 Srinivasa Iyengar, *On Education and Educationists*, pp. 138–9.

20 Ibid.

21 P. Suryanarayana Rao, *The South Indian Teacher*, June 1953.

22 *The Hindu*, 20 July 1953.

were prison houses. Rajaji was out of touch with modern educational trends that had an impact on school education. Schools were now places of joy, freedom and healthy activity.

As Srinivasa Iyengar noted in his book on education in Madras, 'Primary school children in our country were in no way inferior to others in exuberant activity.'[23] The SITU took strong objection to schools being described as prisons.[24] In its journal, *The South Indian Teacher*, it asserted that the school as a social institution came into being only with the purpose of affording to children an amount of education that would enable them to take their place in society. The direction of reform must therefore be towards the strengthening of schools.[25] N. Kuppuswamy Iyengar argued that no one from Pestalozzi to Gandhi had ever suggested that leaving the children to fend for themselves was the remedy. They all wanted to find a way of making teaching interesting so that pupils would feel confinement in school pleasant and agreeable. Rajaji was changing the agreeable simple imprisonment to disagreeable rigorous imprisonment by concentrating all abstract teaching of the three 'R's in 2 hours 40 minutes.[26] The adoption of the shift system, irrespective of the need for it in all classes, would do violence to the conception of the whole school functioning as an indivisible unit to promote corporate activities. The play activities that had become part and parcel of school life would have to be eschewed. Children would have to forego participation in the modern accomplishments of primary education, such as music, drawing, cub scouting, Junior Red Cross and organized play and games. The common assembly of the school which imparted a sense of moral and social life could not be held every day.[27]

[23] Srinivasa Iyengar, *On Education and Educationists*, p. 139.

[24] *The South Indian Teacher*, June 1953, p. 263.

[25] Ibid., p. 264.

[26] *Educational India*, November 1953. Kuppuswamy Iyengar also felt that the new scheme totally neglected inculcation of discipline (*The Hindu*, 4 July 1953).

[27] Srinivasa Iyengar, *On Education and Educationists*, p. 138.

In most rural schools, there was no need for a shift system for the fourth and fifth classes, as the strength would be poor due to dropouts. In rural areas, the greater need was to provide schools in school-less villages. There was no rush into schools to make necessary an assortment into shifts.[28] The critics did not obviously share the optimism of the Education Minister that admissions would get doubled.

The president of the SITU argued that five-hour schooling was based on the principle that abstract subjects should not be taught continuously but interspersed with lighter subjects. Three-hour continuous teaching of abstract subjects would therefore be harmful and futile. The scheme thus violated psychological principles.[29] Further, craft education or training should commence only at the age of ten. It was preposterous to expect six-year-old children to participate in family work. Indeed, at the age of six, the fundamental need of the children was the companionship of other children of their age.[30]

J.C. Kumarappa stated that good craftsmen were seldom good teachers.[31] A large percentage of the population in the village was in no position to give the training contemplated by the scheme. Their own equipment and condition of life militated against the children having a fair deal.[32]

Another educationalist argued that a third of the people in the villages were landless agricultural labourers from whom no craft could be learnt. Given that cultivation was carried on in such a primitive manner there was not much for the children to learn from them every day for three hours; it was therefore meaningless to give to this dubious three-hour contact with parents the high-

28 Ibid.

29 S. Natarajan, President, SITU, *The South Indian Teacher*, May 1953, p. 208.

30 Ibid.

31 J.C. Kumarappa, *The Hindu*, 17 July 1953.

32 S. Natarajan, President, SITU, *The South Indian Teacher*, May 1953, p. 208.

sounding name of craft education. As for blacksmiths, carpenters and cobblers, they were a vanishing tribe in the village as these industries were dying.[33] Further, most work performed by boys was seasonal; the only work done daily was cattle tending which was a full-day occupation. Moreover, boys would have to be at least twelve years before they could participate in such work.[34] It was therefore wrong to expect that the scheme would promote 'dignity of labour'. Village children were not averse to manual work and needed no instruction in the dignity of labour. Indeed, there was a danger that they could become bitter and fall prey to communism if they worked with the parents or observed the parents toiling hard and receiving meagre remuneration in return.[35]

The shift system had been tried elsewhere. In Hyderabad State it had been abandoned as a failure after three years. Shift system required punctuality which could not be expected. Children coming for the second shift often came too early and ended up disturbing the first shift. Parents considered three-hour schooling inadequate.[36] A shift system would not guarantee one hundred per cent enrolment. The experience in Mysore and Rajasthan revealed that there were still 25 to 30 per cent of children whose parents would not enrol them.[37]

The temptation for the parent who wanted to use child labour was to retain the child for the whole day instead of sending him to the afternoon session. Afternoon sessions had low attendance, ending up demoralizing the teacher.[38]

The new scheme ran counter to the UNESCO recommendation

[33] Editorial, *Educational India*, July 1953, p. 22.

[34] N. Kuppuswamy Iyengar, *Educational India*, November 1953, p. 154.

[35] Ibid., p. 153.

[36] Sayidali, ex-Director of Public Instruction, Hyderabad, *Educational India*, October 1953, pp. 104–5.

[37] K.U. Kini, N. Venkatachala Iyengar and Tirunelveli Teachers' Guild, *Educational India*, September 1953 and April 1954.

[38] N. Venkatachala Iyengar, Tirunelveli Teachers' Guild, *The South Indian Teacher*, October 1953, p. 404.

that the minimum content of primary education should be education for five years, consisting of a year of 200 days and a day of 5 hours.[39]

Some of the educationists went beyond what was strictly educational and criticized the socio-economic concepts implied by the scheme.

Rural craftsmen were as eager as others to get for their children what children of upper classes were receiving in schools. Their ambitions could not be manipulated by bigger people; their ideologies could not be cribbed and confined. They would not accept the hereditary role implied in the scheme. It might be madness according to Rajaji to upset the existing structure. But these very communities which the scheme sought to benefit would violently oppose it.[40] N. Kuppuswamy Iyengar asked what was wrong in people aspiring to become government servants when government servants enjoyed benefits denied to the villagers who worked with their hands. His accusation was that the scheme was intended to reduce competition for white-collar jobs by excluding the village children.[41]

The reasons for non-attendance were (1) inaccessibility of schools and lack of transport, (2) poverty of parents who could not provide even slates and books, (3) apathy and indifference due to poor standard of living. But of 17 lakhs of families sending their children to 25,000 rural schools, 15.5 lakhs were of occupational groups and only 1.5 lakhs were of the non-occupational group. This disproved the theory that parents were keeping back the children to help them in their occupation.[42]

The craft training contemplated in the scheme for the age group of 6–11 could hardly solve the unemployment problem. Employment in hereditary or other occupations was determined by the ambitions and aspirations of the people in rural areas, the training given

[39] Srinivasa Iyengar, *On Education and Educationists*, p. 139.

[40] Ibid., p. 132.

[41] *Educational India*, November 1953.

[42] *The South Indian Teacher*, June 1953.

during the 14–18 age period, and by socio-economic development.[43]

Thus, the liberal educationists strongly criticized the scheme as educationally unsound and retrograde. As the SITU pointed out, the scheme, in effect, had limited the objective of elementary education to the mere attainment of literacy and had thrown the responsibility of educating the child in social behaviour and the development of manual skills solely on the parents whereas it was the responsibility of a democratic state to provide for all children as complete an education as possible, and to ensure that the education of no child was limited in any manner either due to poor financial resources or the competence of its parents.[44]

The temper of the educationists could be understood from the demand raised by the president of the District Teachers' Guild of South Arcot that the portfolio of education should be entrusted to a committee of experts and from the statement of one Saraswathy Srinivasan that changes in the system of education should be the work of educationists and not that of the government.[45] It should be noted that most critics of the scheme hailed from the very castes in whose interest, it was claimed, the scheme had been introduced by Rajaji.

EDUCATIONISTS IN SUPPORT

Not all educationists were against the scheme. There were a few who supported it—some because it would spread education; some because its emphasis on craft learning during out-of-school hours would inculcate dignity of labour.

G. Ramachandran, the recently appointed educational advisor to the government, prepared a note titled 'Elementary Schools as They Were', meant for publication and distribution. The note pointed out that more than fifty per cent of children were not on the rolls, and even

[43] Srinivasa Iyengar, *On Education and Educationists*, p. 140.

[44] *The South Indian Teacher*, June 1953, p. 362.

[45] *The South Indian Teacher*, May 1953, p. 206, and October 1953, p. 402.

among the enrolled the wastage was as high as 62 per cent—something 'no nation can sustain for any length of time'. This, compounded by lack of teachers—'in a large majority of 38,000 elementary schools there are not even now as many teachers as there are standards'—resulted 'in strain on the teacher, lack of adequate attention given to children, and consequent inefficiency all around'. More importantly, the long school hours 'stunted the normal growth of body and mind of children, creating in them'—here he borrowed the words of Rajaji—'a drowsiness, haziness and an insufficiency which it is impossible to cure'. The undue emphasis on bookish knowledge turned the minds of children away 'from all physical and manual work as though such work was unconnected with the educational process'.[46]

In August, G. Ramachandran drafted a longer note titled 'The Modified Scheme of Elementary Education: Impressions and Suggestions'.[47] Considerable effort had gone into its writing, for it had been drafted after touring six districts (three in Tamil Nadu) and attending 'crowded meetings of teachers'—he claimed to have met 15,000 teachers and 'spoken to nearly double that number of people at public meetings'—and consulting educational officers and 'many deputations of teachers' associations and numerous leaders of public opinion'. Ramachandran had also had 'some good talks with representatives of the press'.

This note was in three parts: How are the people taking it? How are the teachers taking it? And how are the children taking it?

Considering the first question, Ramachandran had little doubt that the first impression in the minds of rural people was 'one of perplexity'. In their view, reduction of school instruction meant reduction of content of instruction. Many believed that school teachers had conspired to reduce their own workload. He remarked that 'No

[46] This paragraph, based on G.O. No. 1872, Education, 4 August 1953, has been written by the editor.

[47] This section on G. Ramachandran's note, found in G.O. No. 2034, Education, 29 August 1953, has been written by the editor.

one explained to the parents the main features and the advantages of the Modified Scheme. Wherever this is done most difficulties vanish. After all[,] village parents are shrewd people and quite capable of finding out what is good for them'. Evidently, Rajaji's government had not thought it fit to inform the prime stakeholders.

Regarding the general attitude of teachers everywhere, Ramachandran presented 'a complex picture'. While he paid 'tribute to the sense of discipline among the teachers as a whole', it did not amount to saying that 'teachers everywhere were cooperating fully'. The addition of an extra work hour every day and an extra working day every week was far from welcome. Many of the teachers were disgruntled about teaching the same thing twice every day. Ramachandran reassured himself that 'where teachers teach mechanically, all teaching is strain both to themselves and to the children'. Another aspect he noticed was that 'teachers have in some places become "politicals". The department may not have been vigilant enough or strong enough to deal with this situation . . . [T]here are schools where the whole scheme is being deliberately reduced to mockery'. Ramachandran pleaded for greater vigilance in this regard.

Coming to the children themselves, Ramachandran found it 'the most interesting part of the story'. While pupils in the first three standards 'gave a solid vote in favour of the new scheme, children of higher classes were caught up in the same currents as the parents themselves', believing that education comes from more book learning. This, in his view, was 'the tragedy of the situation. The very people who lose most from the earlier order of things have come to love it. Any change upsets them'. Ramachandran, therefore, recommended that things should be explained to the children: 'If it is wrong to give a sense of perplexity to parents, it is even worse to have children perplexed and confused in their minds. Children ought to know what is happening.'

In conclusion, Ramachandran asserted that if the scheme was to succeed, it would require 'much hard work and careful handling' even though he believed that 'we have made a beginning which is fairly good'. 'Careful day to day guidance of teachers is very necessary,' he added.

Though written by an avid advocate of the scheme, Ramachandran's note makes it clear that it was a top-down scheme which had not taken the various stakeholders into confidence. Quite simply, Rajaji knew what was best.

T.V.G. Pal pointed out that, as early as in 1944, a committee consisting of educationists under the chairmanship of Dr A. Lakshmanaswami Mudaliar, had been appointed by the University of Madras to report on the postwar reorganization of education in Madras Presidency and that this committee had recommended a shift system; each shift of four hours, one from 7 to 11 A.M. and the other from 1 to 5 P.M., with a six-day week.[48]

Lt. Col. S. Paul, principal of Guindy Engineering College, considered the Rajaji scheme the nearest and best approach to achieve the objectives of Basic Education. He recalled how his father had adopted a similar scheme as a manager of an estate in Jaffna which ran thirteen Tamil schools and one English school for children of farmers and fishermen—children attended school from 10 A.M. to 1 P.M. only, spending the rest of the day with their working parents. He also cited the example of Singapore where a two–four-hour shift system was adopted with the object of enabling students to assist their parents. The idea was American.[49]

Santhana Krishna Naidu of the Education Department quoted Rousseau and asserted that the child attending the school should not be inferior to the child who did not attend school in respect of skills and abilities naturally and spontaneously acquired from the environment.[50]

K.S. Ramaswami Sastri, noted scholar of Hinduism, welcomed the scheme as it had brought the dream of universal education within

[48] *Swatantra*. [Reference incomplete.—*Ed.*]

[49] *Madras Information*, July 1953.

[50] *Madras Information*, September 1953.

the ambit of reality, without sacrificing efficiency, and had related education to the reality of life and livelihood.[51]

A. Srinivasaraghavan, eminent scholar, poet and principal, V.O.C. College, Tuticorin, commended the scheme as it promoted craft-mindedness.[52] Other notable supporters were Professor N.V. Gadgil,[53] Professor M. Venkatarangaiah,[54] H.D. Rajah,[55] K.C. Sivasami,[56] and Dr Muthulakshmi Reddy.[57]

JURISTIC CRITICISM

Certain critics like V.K. John, S.B. Adithan and Rangaiah pointed out that the scheme violated international conventions on child rights as no definite line could be drawn between acquiring skill through participation in work and effective employment in production. The child would have to do work which was neither conducive to its health and development nor appropriate for its age. The scheme implicitly approved child labour and was contrary to the spirit of the Constitution (Article 24) which disapproved the employment of children under the age of fourteen years.[58]

In their view, the scheme had simply accepted the reality of child labour which would persist in rural areas whether the scheme was in force or not. Further, the Minimum Age (Agriculture) Convention, 1921 provided that children under the age of fourteen years shall not be employed or work in any public or private agricultural undertaking save outside school hours. However, the children could be employed for purposes of practical vocational training subject to

[51] *The South Indian Teacher*, October 1953.

[52] Ibid.

[53] *The Hindu*, 7 June 1953.

[54] *The Hindu*, 3 June 1953.

[55] *The Hindu*, 10 July 1953.

[56] *The Hindu*, 21 July 1953.

[57] *The Hindu*, 29 July 1953.

[58] Ibid.

certain restrictions.[59] The International Labour Organization (ILO) convention thus permitted child labour subject to the condition that the school education of the child was not affected. (India had not ratified this convention.)

The basic cause for children to work was the poverty of the family and until poverty was eradicated child labour would persist, for which drastic socio-economic changes would have to take place. Until then, what the poor working child could hope for, and what the state should try to provide was only part-time schooling. This has been recognized in England a century ago as noted earlier. Further under the scheme, children in the first two standards were only to observe and not work, and in higher standards their participation was in the nature of apprenticeship.

POLITICIANS

The initial reaction of political parties took the form of verbal criticism through the press and at public meetings. Later it took an agitational turn when the Dravidar Kazhagam (DK) and the Dravida Munnetra Kazhagam (DMK) entered the fray. The scheme blew into a major political issue following the debate in the legislature. A further stage of politicization of the issue was reached, in what one might call a second round of battle, after the partition of Madras State and the submission of the Parulekar Committee Report (PCR). The PCR rekindled the controversy among educationists over aspects of educational philosophy and practice. But by then the political struggle against Rajaji had begun to overshadow all other issues.

Confined to the initial phase of criticism, this section discusses the educational and socio-economic philosophies behind the criticisms levelled by various political groups.

The DK, led by Periyar E.V. Ramasamy, was the first to condemn the scheme. Its organ *Viduthalai* published a letter from A. Vyapuri,

[59] Quoted in M.L. Pandhe (ed.), *Child Labour in India*, p. 17.

secretary of Salem Dravidian Teachers' Union, warning of the danger of the new scheme.[60] Soon, it reported a speech by Rajaram Naidu at Virudhunagar containing a hint of the 'revolutionary' changes in the educational system being contemplated by Rajaji.[61] After the publication of the scheme, *Viduthalai* gave extensive coverage to criticisms of the scheme from all quarters. The scheme was dubbed '*Varnashrama* Education Scheme' and then '*Kula Kalvi Thittam*' (caste-based education scheme)—a name that stuck. A resolution to carry on an agitation against the scheme was passed at the Tiruchi Taluk Dravidian Agricultural Workers Conference, in which Periyar EVR participated.[62] It was argued that the scheme would perpetuate the caste system and deny the lower castes the opportunity to take to other professions. It was a conspiracy of the Brahmins to keep down the Non-Brahmins. Rajaji had always been acting in the interests of the Brahmins and was inimical to the interests of the Non-Brahmins.

Periyar EVR listed out the various anti-Non-Brahmin acts of Rajaji during both his regimes: 1937–39 and 1952–54. The long list included the reduction of the education cess in 1937–39 thereby depriving district boards of the resources for running schools, the abolition of secondary schools with a strength of less than 60 pupils, the closure of Forest College, the closure of 'uneconomical' elementary schools (2,500 in 1937–39 and 6,000 in 1952–54), the withdrawal of educational concessions to Scheduled Caste converts to Christianity, the introduction of Basic Education and now, finally, the Kula Kalvi Thittam.[63] Thus, the Kula Kalvi Thittam was seen by Periyar EVR as an integral part of the consistently anti-Non-Brahmin policy of a casteist Rajaji.

The DMK endorsed the view of the DK that the scheme was based on *varnashrama dharma*, so dear to Rajaji's heart, and was

[60] *Viduthalai*, 7 April 1953.

[61] *Viduthalai*, 13 April 1953.

[62] *Viduthalai*, 21 June 1953.

[63] Periyar EVR, *Achariar Atchiyin Kodumaigal*.

intended to perpetuate the privileges of the upper castes, particularly the Brahmins.[64]

The Communist Party of India, then the main Opposition party in the state legislature, considered the scheme an ugly attempt to preserve the status quo in the socio-economic life of rural society by forcing the children to stick to their ancestral crafts, thus attempting to ensure that the poor did not get much education and start demanding jobs, which was then the preserve of others. Unlike the DK and the DMK, the Communists did not accuse Rajaji of casteist motivation but opposed the scheme as retrograde because it tried to take the country back to a pre-industrial age. They wondered how the steady destruction of the life process in the village could be arrested by an educational scheme when its causes were socio-economic, requiring a change in the very foundation of the economic system of the country. What prevented poor children from attending schools was poverty of their parents which required a solution first.[65] The need of the hour was to replace the feudal-colonial set-up by a healthy, national, independent, socially-planned, productive modern economy. Education then should be science-based and science-oriented.[66] The Communists also contended that the scheme increased the workload of teachers. If the government were really sincere in spreading education, they would have recruited more teachers apart from improving the teacher's lot.[67]

The Indian Socialist Party, led by Dr K.B. Menon in the legislature, also opposed the scheme. Dignity of labour was a social product arising from certain social and economic conditions. Until suitable conditions were created, dignity of labour could not be instilled

64 *Manram*, 1 July 1953.

65 Speeches of T. Nagi Reddy and M. Kalyanasundaram, *Madras Legislative Assembly Debates*, vol. IX, 29 July 1953, pp. 1724 and 1728.

66 P. Ramamurthi, *Madras Legislative Assembly Debates*, vol. IX, 15 July 1953, pp. 145–7.

67 M. Kalyanasundaram, *Madras Legislative Assembly Debates*, 29 July 1953, pp. 1725–9.

whatever be the kind of education.[68] The Socialist Party passed a resolution condemning the scheme as anti-worker and anti-peasant, and demanded its immediate withdrawal.[69]

Other constituents of the United Democratic Front, the alliance of Opposition parties, particularly the Tamil Nadu Toilers' Party, also opposed the scheme vehemently. A. Govindaswami Nayagar of the Tamil Nadu Toilers' Party pointed out that the scheme violated the constitutional safeguard that protected children and the youth from exploitation, and from moral and material abandonment (Article 39 (f) of the Constitution of India).[70] S.C.C. Anthony Pillai wondered how the extra two hours a day the child was going to remain with the parent would make any difference in the attitude of the child that the nineteen hours a day the child was already spending with its parents could not inculcate.[71] Tenneti Viswanatham called it a 'wandering scheme'.[72] S.P. Thangavelu and two Scheduled Caste legislators, A. Rathinam and M. Dharmalingam, feared that children of the depressed castes would be greatly affected, as they would have to remain cowherds.[73] V.R. Nagarajan questioned why the scheme was not extended to urban areas if it was really educationally sound.[74]

The ruling Congress party, for its part, was a house divided. From the outset, K. Kamaraj was opposed to the scheme, who considered it as little more than an attempt to cover up financial expediency.[75] However, once he realized that anti-Congress forces were taking advantage of the issue, he restricted himself to inner-party activity. Omandur P. Ramaswamy Reddiar, former premier of Madras, in

[68] *Madras Legislative Assembly Debates*, 29 July 1953. Also, *Swatantra*, 13 June 1953, pp. 46–7.

[69] *Dravida Nadu*, 26 July 1953.

[70] *Madras Legislative Assembly Debates*, 29 July 1953, vol. IX.

[71] Ibid., pp. 1705–7.

[72] Ibid., pp. 1713–14.

[73] Ibid., pp. 1715–16; 1717–18; 1718–19.

[74] Ibid.

[75] *The Hindu*, 21 June 1953.

whose period the shift system was introduced in schools on optional basis, pointed out that with the serious rural unemployment and poverty that prevailed, the scheme was unworkable.[76]

Similar views were expressed by T. Chengalvarayan, Dr P. Subbarayan, former chief minister, and T.S. Avinashilingam Chettiar, former education minister.[77] R.S. Arumugam, a Congress MLA with twelve years of experience as elementary school teacher, spoke against the scheme in the legislature. He pointed out that the children of a family went to school together and therefore the shift system would cause them great inconvenience.[78]

The opposition to the scheme from the Congress legislators was so strong that a whip had to be issued to vote against the Opposition resolution on 29 July 1953. At the meeting of the Congress legislative party on the eve of the voting, G. Ramachandran was pressed into service to explain the virtues of the scheme but it cut no ice. It was only political expediency—the necessity to save the government of the day—that forced the party to give qualified support to the scheme.[79]

THE DEFENCE

Against the combined onslaught of so many diverse forces, Rajaji defended his scheme as ably as he could. To the teachers he gave an

[76] *The Hindu*, 19 June 1953.

[77] Speech of R.S. Arumugam, *Madras Legislative Assembly Debates*, vol. IX, 29 July 1953, p. 1720–21.

[78] *Madras Legislative Assembly Debates*, 1953, vol. IX, p. 1720. R.S. Arumugam had stated that the Tamil Nadu Congress Committee (TNCC) had proposed an alternative to the scheme. Probably he was referring to the resolution of the TNCC Executive Committee which had pointed out how the enemies of the Congress were exploiting the issue and suggested the adoption of the shift system until facilities could be made available to introduce Basic Education to which the Congress was committed. The Committee recommended to the government to redress the grievances of the teachers (Minutes of the Executive Committee, Congress Office, Teynampet).

[79] *The Hindu*, 28 July 1953.

assurance that there would be no retrenchment.[80] He tried to convince them that their workload would in fact be reduced, especially in single-teacher schools, as a teacher then handling two classes simultaneously would thereafter have to handle only one class in each shift.[81]

Rajaji made a concession in regard to the out-of-school-hour programme, making it optional. A further climbdown was when he argued that the touchstone for examining the measure should be whether every boy would become literate, whether more people would be benefited, instead of the existing state of affairs in which only a section of the community got education. The main aspect of his scheme was the reduction of school hours. Thus, he retreated from his earlier stand that the greatest merit of the scheme was the out-of-school apprenticeship programme and that universalization was just a by-product. He also defended the utilization of village craftsmen. Dr Zakir Husain had admitted in his letter to Rajaji that the work programme in Basic-trained teachers lacked drive, earnestness, and sincerity. By trying to mobilize village artisans for the work of education, Dr Husain felt that Rajaji had taken a very vital step in the right direction.[82] Rajaji asked why we should not consider the whole village as a school—as a polytechnic of cottage industries.[83] In order to counter the propaganda that the scheme perpetuated the caste system, the children were given freedom to opt for a craft other than their parents' craft. Rajaji asked how the scheme could be detrimental to the interests of the downtrodden when the only opportunity they had to get themselves educated was part-time schooling. To the criticism that the rural areas were discriminated against, his answer

[80] C. Subramaniam, *Madras Legislative Assembly Debates*, 1954, vol. XIII, p. 1154.

[81] *Madras Legislative Assembly Debates*, vol. X, 24 December 1953, p. 734. Rajaji called the existing state of affairs a 'fraud'. Kalyanasundaram retorted that the fraud was the government's, which failed to provide a teacher for every class (ibid., p. 744).

[82] *Madras Legislative Assembly Debates*, vol. IX, 29 July 1953, p. 1738.

[83] Ibid., p. 1736.

was to announce an extension of the scheme to major *panchayats* and urban areas.[84]

The Education Department took active steps to sell the scheme to teachers. The Inspectors of Schools attended the meetings of the teachers' guilds at all district centres. The Opposition charged the Education Department with using coercive measures to compel unwilling local authorities to introduce the scheme. Only one *panchayat* in the state stood firm till the end, refusing to introduce the scheme in its schools.[85]

Kalki, the eponymous weekly edited by the popular nationalist writer and journalist Kalki R. Krishnamurthy, known for his unquestioning devotion to Rajaji, carried on a polemical campaign in support of the scheme. It referred to a spate of suicides by students who had failed in the examinations and condemned the system of education that created in them an inferiority complex that they were good-for-nothing if they failed in the examinations. Such a system of education was really a 'killer' education.[86] The new scheme would create self-reliant, self-confident citizens. *Kalki* decried school education and emphasized that respect for physical work alone had made America great. Lincoln was a woodcutter, Krishna a shepherd, Tiruvalluvar a weaver, while Vedanta Desikar cobbled.[87] It rejected the charge that the scheme would perpetuate the caste system. On the contrary, it was the old system that perpetuated the caste system by denying opportunities for education to the lower castes. Under the new scheme, a blacksmith's son could become a district collector and a washerman's son a lawyer, as every child would have schooling.[88] Children of all castes would not only learn the three 'R's together but also a craft. The arrangement of family apprenticeship suggested in

84 This was done after the publication of the PCR.

85 *Madras Legislative Assembly Debates*, 1954, vol. XIV, p. 167.

86 *Kalki*, 14 June 1953.

87 *Kalki*, 7 June 1953.

88 *Kalki*, 28 June 1953.

Viduthalai, 27 July 1953.

'The New Education Scheme.'

The Aryan boy is being taught to read by his mother while the Dravidian boy is riding a bullock. Rajaji's dream comes true!

the scheme was only in recognition of the reality as it existed in the villages.[89] It had no evil motives as attributed to it by the opponents.

In the face of mounting opposition, Rajaji responded by organizing a conference of education officers at the secretariat during 1–3 June.[90] Apart from all officers of the Education Department and the presidents of district boards (who, as local government, managed the schools), the conference was attended by the Chief Minister in

89 *Kalki*, July 1953.

90 This paragraph (written by the editor) is based on the 'Note on Modified Scheme' in G.O. No. 1872, Education, 4 August 1953.

the company of some of his ministers. The opening statement by the Education Minister flagged the salient features of the scheme and defended it. The DPI outlined the magnitude of the scheme: while there were 21,784 primary schools with 2,937,277 pupils, and 92,168 teachers, he sought to 'belie the fears of critics', stating that only 10,875 schools needed to be equipped to handle the occupational training needs as the rest had 'already secured promise of help from farmers and craftsmen'. At the end of the first day's session, Rajaji himself addressed the conference, allaying fears of retrenchment of teachers. Refuting the criticism that young children would be made to do 'unpleasant work', he clarified that 'the scheme merely aimed to habituate the children to the circumstances and atmosphere of work, and not to give them occupational training'. Clearly Rajaji was tinkering with the objectives of the scheme as originally enunciated to make it more acceptable. On the second day of the conference, the Chief Minister preferred to discuss practical issues regarding implementation rather than elaborate on the philosophy and objectives of the scheme. At the end of the conference, it was decided that the scheme would cover all major [Class I] *panchayats* (but municipalities, i.e. towns and cities, would be left out) rather than be restricted to rural areas alone as stated at the outset.

But even by July 1953—within months of its announcement and weeks of its implementation—Rajaji was forced to go on the defensive and to make concessions which seriously compromised his original stand. This was mainly due to the turn the controversy took following the agitations by the DK and DMK.

THE 'AGITATIONAL' PHASE

Soon after the commencement of the new school year, a 'protest day' was observed on 21 June 1953 in response to the call of the DK and the DMK.[91] The next phase of the agitation was to present

[91] T.M. Parthasarathy, *Ti.Mu.Ka. Varalaru*, p. 205.

Viduthalai, 1 August 1953.

'The Students are to Learn a Hereditary Occupation.'

Teacher: 'What's your father's occupation?' Student: 'Bootlegging, Sir!'

The elementary school teacher, following Rajaji's advice, is looking for a place to impart vocational training!

memoranda to the members of legislature in each constituency from 8 July 1953 onwards. A DK procession in the city of Madras tried to enter the Government Estate on 14 July 1953 for the ostensible purpose of meeting the MLAs, violating the prohibitory order then in force. V. Veerasami, MP and others were arrested and the procession dispersed by the use of force.[92]

The DMK had, as part of their 'three-pronged struggle'[93]

[92] *Madras Legislative Assembly Debates*, 1953, vol. IX, p. 465.

[93] The 'three-pronged' agitation of the DMK was to protest against (1) the

(*mummunai porattam*), resolved to picket the Chief Minister's residence on 14 July 1953. Adjournment motions on the arrest were disallowed by the Speaker of the legislative assembly.[94] The three-pronged agitation took a violent turn at Tuticorin and Kallakudi (near Trichy) with the police resorting to firing on 15 July 1953. Following these events, a tense atmosphere prevailed all over the state.[95]

The DK carried on a campaign of picketing elementary schools on 20 July 1953. A large number of picketing volunteers were arrested all over the state. This was followed by protest marches at various centres to publicize the evils of the scheme. On 24 July 1953, Periyar addressed a mammoth gathering in Madras city. The DMK agitation continued till the end of the July session of the Assembly. The situation deteriorated so rapidly that the MSEE was no longer an educational issue debated by educationists in a calm atmosphere but a political issue charged with emotion.

THE POLITICAL BATTLE

Following the arrest of the DMK leaders, the Opposition in the legislature raised the issue of the education scheme on 15 July 1953.[96] Rajaji had his own priorities. He refused to take up this issue until the house completed its deliberation on the bill for the separation of Andhra State.

The education scheme was taken up for discussion only on 29 July 1953 towards the end of the Assembly session. Even here, Rajaji saw to it that the Opposition motions were not taken up. Only the government motion was debated. The Opposition had to be content with moving amendments to the motion. A large number

education scheme, (2) the naming of Kallakudi railway station after the Marwari businessman Dalmia as Dalmiapuram, and (3) Nehru's remark that the DMK agitation was 'nonsense'.

94 *The Hindu*, 14 July 1953.

95 *Viduthalai*, 21 July to 31 July 1953.

96 *The Hindu*, 25 July 1953.

of amendments were moved.[97] The Speaker classified them into two categories: one—of which the Communist member K.P.R. Gopalan's was typical—adding the words 'on such consideration, the assembly recommends to the government that the scheme be dropped'; and the other—of which that of the Tamil Nadu Toilers' Party's K.R. Viswanathan's was typical—substituting for the words 'taken to consideration' the words 'stayed and referred to an expert committee of officials and non-officials in the educational field'. After a heated four-hour debate, K.P.R. Gopalan's amendment was declared lost after the Speaker cast his vote against it. C. Subramaniam opposed putting Viswanathan's amendment to vote arguing that 'dropped' and 'stayed' had the same meaning. The Speaker accepted Nagi Reddy's clarification that 'dropped' meant giving up the scheme once and for all while 'stayed' meant only a temporary suspension with the option to take up the scheme after the expert committee's examination. Viswanathan's amendment was finally carried with 139 votes for and 137 votes against. An independent MLA, H. Siddanna Gowd, had crossed over to the Opposition.[98] The legislative council, however, supported the government and rejected the Opposition's motions.

The next day Tenneti Viswanatham, T. Prakasam's right-hand man, tried first to raise a point of order on the legality of Rajaji's government continuing after the defeat in the legislature. When this was ruled out, he tried to move a privilege motion, which too was not allowed. Rajaji held that the resolution adopted by the legislature was only recommendatory, citing precedents in British parliamentary practice to justify his refusal to resign. He challenged the Opposition to move a no-confidence motion if they wanted him out of office.[99]

The first round of battle thus ended only in a partial victory for the Opposition. It could not dislodge Rajaji's government, their real

[97] *Madras Legislative Assembly Debates*, 1953, vol. IX, p. 145.

[98] Ibid., p. 1739.

[99] Proceedings of 30 July 1953, *Madras Legislative Assembly Debates*, 1953, vol. IX, p. 665.

objective. Nor could it bring about the withdrawal of the scheme or even its suspension, for Rajaji did not adopt this part of the 'recommendation'. Meanwhile, the DMK suspended its agitation.[100] But the DK continued its campaign.

100 Parthasarathy, *Ti.Mu.Ka. Varalaru*, p. 243.

CHAPTER III

THE SECOND ROUND OF BATTLE

LEGAL QUIBBLING

Following the passage of the Opposition amendment in the legislative assembly directing that the Modified Scheme of Elementary Education (MSEE) be stayed and referred to an experts' committee, and the rejection of the Opposition motion in the legislative council, which was on the same lines as the amendment passed by the Assembly, Rajaji took shelter under Dicey's dictum. According to its terms, a resolution in the nature of obtaining an opinion so as to assist the government in framing of government policy was not a law. His government was therefore free to decide and had therefore decided that any change at that stage would interrupt and disturb the working of the schools. Instead, he announced that an expert committee would be appointed to appraise results. If the Assembly desired strict adherence to the letter of the resolution, he added, it would have to take steps to place some other government in power. He thus challenged the Opposition to move a separate motion of no-confidence.[1]

C. Subramaniam, who took over the education portfolio after the formation of Andhra State, confirmed that the scheme 'stayed where it was on the date the assembly passed the resolution', which meant that the scheme stood at the stage when it had been introduced and was therefore in force.[2]

On 20 August 1953 the government appointed a committee under the chairmanship of Professor R.V. Parulekar to examine the

[1] *Madras Legislative Council Debates*, 1953, vol. V, July 1953, p. 665.

[2] *Madras Legislative Assembly Debates*, 1953, vol. X, p. 375.

scheme.[3] The other members of the committee were Dr B.B. Dey, retired Director of Public Instruction (DPI), Madras, M. Mujeeb, Vice-Chancellor, Jamia Millia Islamia, Delhi with S. Govindarajulu, DPI acting as member-secretary of the Committee.[4]

The appointment of the expert committee as early as August 1953 was itself a great concession on the part of Rajaji to the Opposition, for he had till then asserted that no review of the scheme could be undertaken until it had been in operation for at least a year.[5]

The composition of the Committee came in for severe criticism from the Opposition. Given that there was not a single non-official educationist belonging to the state on the Committee, Rajaji was accused of packing the Committee with his supporters.[6]

To a question in the legislative assembly by A. Govindaswami Nayagar, 'why no prominent educationist from Tamilnad was included', C. Subramaniam, asserting that members were chosen 'on the basis of the high standing . . . as Educationists', added, with little conviction, that 'Dr B.B. Dey, . . . was the Director of Public Instruction for a number of years in the Composite Madras State' and that 'Sri S. Govindarajulu Naidu, the Member-Secretary of the Committee, belongs to Madras'. When, the Member, in a supplementary asked

[3] Rajaji had 'earnestly requested' Dr Zakir Husain to serve on the committee but he declined pleading 'ill-health and congestion of work' as vice-chancellor of Aligarh Muslim University. This is stated in Rajaji's letter to Professor M. Mujeeb of Jamia Millia Islamia. G.O. No. 1988, Education, 20 August 1953.—*Ed.*

[4] G.O. No. 1988, Education, 20 August 1953.

[5] Rajaji commented (on 30 July 1953) in a government file that 'Government will give due consideration to the view expressed in the house', but emphasized that it was 'most undesirable . . . to interrupt and disturb the working of the schools in the middle of the year. Government have already assured the Opposition that an expert committee will be appointed in due course to appraise the results and make its considered recommendations'. G.O. No. 1988, Education, 20 August 1953.—*Ed.*

[6] Speeches of V.R. Nagarajan and T.C. Narayana Nambiar, *Madras Legislative Assembly Debates*, 1953, vol. X, pp. 164 and 719.

if Parulekar was made the chair of the Committee only because he would approve the half-a-day school system, he replied, 'No, Sir, as an educationist, and as one who has done some work in the field of elementary education.'[7] He went further and stated: 'As a matter of fact we did not know the Chairman of the Committee before. We did not know who he was'—a statement which can only be said to belong to the category of Churchill-ian terminological inexactitudes.[8]

THE PARULEKAR COMMITTEE REPORT (PCR)

The Parulekar Committee held its first sitting on 31 August 1953.[9] It visited some schools around Madras and found that the schools were only then beginning to understand the implications of the scheme and trying to adjust themselves to it. It thought that no useful purpose would be served by going around the state and visiting more schools. It, therefore, decided to examine the scheme on its educational and practical aspects on the basis of knowledge of educational theory and practice that its members possessed.[10]

The Committee's exercise was thus purely theoretical. The report submitted to the government on 23 November 1953 was more or less the expert opinion of Parulekar whose programmes for the universalization of elementary education were already well known. The PCR was accepted by the government and published immediately.[11]

[7] This point is based on G.O. No. 1167, Education, 16 August 1954, and has been written by the editor.

[8] *Madras Legislative Assembly Debates*, 1953, vol. X, p. 377. It is inconceivable that Rajaji did not know about Parulekar whose proposals were what he had commented upon in 1949 as governor-general.

[9] The Committee sat on the following days: 31 August – 5 September; 24–30 September; and 14 October – 2 November 1953. G.O. No. 1167, Education, 16 August 1954.—*Ed.*

[10] See 'Introduction', *Report of the Committee on Elementary Education in Madras, 1953.*

[11] G.O. No. 2574, Education, 26 November 1953. 5,000 copies were printed, 3,900 copies of which were available for public sale (G.O. No. 1303,

The PCR contained a detailed survey of the progress of elementary education in Madras State from 1920 to 1952, focusing especially on the progress of the universalization of education.[12] It concluded that the MSEE was very similar to the shift system, with the difference that a programme of activity during the hours spent outside the school was added to it. In its view the scheme was educationally sound.[13] It approached the question on the presumption that the scheme was intended to enable the existing teachers to teach more children—theoretically double the number of children then at school.[14] It suggested minor modifications to the number of periods to be allotted to core subjects to facilitate study of optional subjects.[15] Three hours of schooling was considered adequate. It wanted a new atmosphere favourable to increased enrolment to be created without delay if the objective to increase the enrolment was to be achieved.[16] Increased salary to the teachers was one of the essential prerequisites for creating the right atmosphere.[17] It recommended an increase in pupil–teacher ratio from the existing 30:1 to 50:1 in two or three years.[18]

It felt that the 'big programme' outside the school being largely left to take care of itself was not desirable and that arrangements should be made for the supervision of the out-of-school programme by enlisting the services of helpers on honorary or paid basis.[19] It suggested material incentives to be given to the craftsmen who were utilized to teach the children.[20] Since village craftsmen would often be uninstructed in scientific methods of work and in handling children, a scheme for training the craftsmen in the art of instructing children

Education, 13 September 1954).—*Ed.*

12 *Report of the Committee on Elementary Education in Madras*, pp. 1–9.

13 Ibid., p. 10.

14 Ibid., p. 18.

15 Ibid., p. 13.

16 Ibid., p. 38.

17 Ibid., p. 46.

18 Ibid., p. 48.

19 Ibid., p. 54.

20 Ibid., p. 55.

காமதேனுவின் மேல் கல்லெறி !

Kalki, 26 July 1953.

'Throwing Stones at the Kamadhenu.'

The new education scheme is the Kamadhenu while its opponents are mischievous boys throwing stones at it. The common man suggests that government provide full-time schooling to them.

needed to be drawn up and implemented.[21] In short, the out-of-school programme required greater care than was contemplated in the scheme. Conditions were also to be created for the community to step in and fulfil the idea.[22] Another recommendation related to the revision of the curriculum which had become out of date.

The committee also recommended a provision for the whole school to be together at least for two full days in the month, increased emoluments and incentives to teachers, alternating between difficult and easy subjects, extension of the scheme to urban areas, provision for scouting and Junior Red Cross, housing for teachers, etc.[23]

[21] Ibid., p. 56.
[22] Ibid., p. 59.
[23] Ibid., p. 60.

Accepting the Parulekar Committee's report, the DPI recommended that the scheme be extended to municipal areas by the next academic year (commencing June 1954) as well. The problem with this was that the out-of-school programme would have to be different. In towns and cities 'there can be no agricultural work . . . and the conditions in which craftsmen and tradesmen work . . . are different'. Further, the DPI recommended its extension to primary sections of secondary schools as well. Towards the 'speedy and successful implementation of the recommendation', the DPI asked for additional staff. The government duly approved it. Evidently, Rajaji was digging his heels in, rather than heeding the snowballing criticism.[24]

In fact, Rajaji went one step further. He chose to implement the recommendation of the Parulekar Committee to revise 'the existing curriculum for elementary schools [which] was brought into effect nearly fifteen years ago . . . [since] changes have taken place since then in educational theory and practice, and also in view of the attempt to provide universal elementary education through the Modified Scheme, it has become necessary to revise the curriculum without delay'. A committee was constituted for this purpose which included the DPI, G. Ramachandran and some teachers.[25]

The Rajaji government contended that the Parulekar Committee's finding was that the scheme was

> educationally sound and offered a practical solution to the problem of carrying out the directives of the Constitution. The Committee has made 22 recommendations covering the three aspects . . . shortened work hours, the two daily sessions and the out-of-school programme. Such of the recommendations of the Committee like flexibility of school hours, constitution of village

[24] This paragraph (written by the editor) is based on G.O. No. 2617, Education, 7 December 1953.

[25] This paragraph (written by the editor) is based on G.O. No. 2863, Education, 26 December 1953.

school councils etc. which do not involve any large financial commitments have been accepted.[26]

The PCR rekindled controversy among the educationists, which had been pushed to the background due to the politicization of the issue. Before we consider the reactions to the report, the action taken on it by the Rajaji government, and its ultimate abandonment by the Kamaraj government, it is necessary to consider the drastic change in the political scene following the separation of Andhra from Madras State.

THE FORMATION OF ANDHRA STATE AND AFTER

Following the decision of the Union government to create a separate state of Andhra, a bill for the bifurcation of the composite Madras State was introduced in the state legislature. Rajaji proved himself to be an intense Tamil nationalist and succeeded in thwarting the attempts of the Andhra State to have Madras city as a common capital of the two states and in retaining Madras city as the capital of the residuary state.[27] His determination to see through the Andhra State Bill was so great that he refused to take up for discussion the education scheme until the Andhra State Bill was passed.

With the passing of the Andhra State Bill, and the inauguration of the new state on 1 October 1953, Rajaji's mission was over. The Congress now had a comfortable majority in the Assembly. There was no longer any threat to the government from anti-Congress forces as in 1952 when Prakasam and the United Democratic Front were ready to assume power. The Congress party could now breathe freely.

Ever since Rajaji had assumed power in April 1952, the

[26] This paragraph (written by the editor) is based on G.O. No. 1167, Education, 16 August 1954.

[27] See Prologue of current volume for a more nuanced discussion on this statement by Veeraraghavan, pp. 37–41.—*Ed.*

Congress legislators had felt cramped. They could not interfere in the administration in any way. Nor were they able to even take up the grievances of their constituents with the officials. Since 1946, they had been accustomed to certain influence and authority in the government offices. Rajaji had blocked all opportunity for the exercise of such power.

Moves to oust Rajaji had been made by Congress men as early as in April 1953.[28] *Kalki* demanded that before they asked Rajaji to step down they elect a replacement unanimously. *Ananda Vikatan* condemned the attempts to sow dissensions within the Congress over the education scheme and commended the speech of Rajaji at the Saidapet political conference in July 1953 in which he had elaborated on the responsibilities of the leader of the party and of the leader of the government, and the relations that should prevail between them.[29]

By October 1953, the anti-Rajaji activities inside the Congress gathered momentum, thanks to the efforts of Dr P. Varadarajulu Naidu and K.T. Kosalram who had been personally affected by certain decisions of Rajaji. Rajaji tried to render powerless the opposition within the Congress by expanding his ministry and roping in supporters of Kamaraj. But the inclusion of Jothi Venkatachalam in the cabinet was resented by the Kamaraj faction.[30] The Congress suffered a defeat in the by-election in Kangeyam. The Opposition claimed that this was a vote against the education scheme.[31] But *Kalki* accused the Tamil Nadu Congress Committee (TNCC) of wanton negligence in conducting the election campaign.[32] The anti-Rajaji elements conducted a signature campaign. Jawaharlal Nehru, however, advised against any change in leadership.[33] The campaigners were rebuffed by the Congress high command which rejected their charges against

28 *Kalki*, 12 April 1953.

29 *Ananda Vikatan*, 2 August 1953.

30 *Swatantra*, 14 November 1953; *Viduthalai*, 1 November 1953.

31 *Dravida Nadu*, 15 November 1953.

32 *Kalki*, 22 November 1953.

33 *Viduthalai*, 1 November 1953.

Rajaji. Kamaraj, as TNCC president, was also reported to have met Rajaji and asked him to resign.[34] Rajaji was firm that it would not be in the interests of the country for him to leave before alternate arrangements were made, and a new leader named and accepted by the people.[35] Rajaji's moves to abolish the Revenue Board and the district boards were frustrated by the Congress party.[36]

The acrimonious campaign would have disgusted any person. The Congress dissident campaign went on even within the legislature, contrary to all conventions that members of the ruling party be restrained in their criticism of the government. Kosalram, a close associate of Kamaraj, characterized the Rajaji government as '*peyatchi*' (Devil's Rule), and levelled serious allegations, of favouritism, casteism and interference in the working of the judiciary, against Rajaji.[37] The Kamaraj faction, which controlled the TNCC, virtually treated Rajaji's government like an Opposition government.

Rajaji was bitter. Speaking on the education demand, he said,

> It is our misfortune in this state that the feelings with regard to the castes and communities are so strong and are such an obsession . . . the matter (MSEE) has been made into a political issue, a political debate, a furious debate very close to a communal debate, a communal issue and there are people who thrive on this kind of misrepresentation.[38]

Rajaji decided to quit office after the Budget session. He sent his resignation on 26 March 1954.

Swiftly, the Congress legislative party decided to drop the education scheme by an overwhelming majority. Kamaraj was elected

34 *Dravida Nadu*, 3 January 1954. Rajaji, in a statement on 3 November 1953, called the dissidents power seekers and vowed not to yield to them.

35 *Ananda Vikatan*, 11 November 1953.

36 *Viduthalai*, 15 December 1953.

37 *Madras Legislative Assembly Debates*, 1953, vol. X, p. 165.

38 Ibid., pp. 716–8.

leader of the Congress legislative party defeating C. Subramaniam by 93 votes to 41.[39] Thus ended the interlude of Rajaji in the post-Independence history of Tamil Nadu. Kamaraj was in command again, this time not as the kingmaker but as the king himself. The irony was that the very forces that had stalled Kamaraj in 1952 were now instrumental in his return to power.

If the first round of battle for the dislodgement of Rajaji from the chief ministership was fought by the anti-Congress opposition, the second round of battle was fought within, with the Dravidar Kazhagam's agitation continuing outside, more in the manner of drum beaters. The common feature of both the rounds of conflict was that casteism was the ammunition used. A new era in the politics of Tamil Nadu was ushered in. The long-range effects of the events of 1953–54 continue to be felt till today.

CAUSE OF RAJAJI'S FALL

Before we return to the main story—the fate of the education scheme—let us analyse briefly the causes that led to Rajaji's fall. Rajaji's re-entry into Tamil Nadu politics was at a time when the prestige of the Congress was at its nadir. As noted earlier, the manner in which he was brought in to head the government was far from democratic. Had Rajaji got himself elected to the legislative assembly on assuming office, the stigma of backdoor entry through the legislative council would not have stuck.[40] But his disdain for the masses was such that he would not subject himself to the electoral process. This condescending attitude was exhibited in his relations with the party and partymen. They had requested him to lead them. Once his leadership was accepted, their business was over. They had only to place complete confidence in him and give him full rein in running affairs. They had no right even to demand consultation, not to speak of interfering in

39 *Viduthalai*, 31 March 1954.

40 K.T. Kosalram, *Madras Legislative Assembly Debates*, 1953, vol. X, p. 166.

what he did or advising him. Rajaji went to the extent of comparing himself to Sankara and Ramanuja, and asked if these *acharyas* acted only after consulting their disciples.[41] This analogy was of course out of place in a political democracy.

Rajaji had not established, and did not make any serious effort to create, a mass base among the rank and file of the Congress.[42] He depended on the respect he commanded among the national leaders of the Congress. The national leadership, with all their prestige and authority, could do little to rehabilitate him in the Tamil Nadu Congress from whom Rajaji had stood alienated since 1942. During this momentous decade, Kamaraj had built the party and its character had also undergone a sea change after Independence. It was less an organization of selfless fighters and more of an establishment. Rajaji could not work with this kind of establishment; nor could he change it as he could never be within it. Quit he had to in the end; quit he did finally when he founded the Swatantra Party in 1959.

As chief minister, Rajaji took many bold decisions which found mass acceptance. The de-control of food, the Tanjore Tenant and Pannaiyal Protection Bill, the Tanjore Tenancy Regulations, his defence of the interests of the handloom weavers—all had created mass goodwill. A social conservative, averse to radical socio-economic changes, he was deeply committed to the preservation of traditional rural society.[43]

The traditional rural society was based on *varnashrama dharma* in which the Brahmin caste enjoyed the highest status. His defence of the traditional rural society, even if on purely socio-economic considerations, could easily be assailed as an attempt to preserve Brahmin domination.[44] It was therefore quite natural for the Dravidar Kazhagam (DK) and the Dravida Munnetra Kazhagam (DMK) to exploit fully this aspect of his philosophy as expressed in the education

41 *Viduthalai*, 31 May 1953 (report from the *Swadesamitran*).

42 Aruna Sivakami, 'Rajaji: A Study in Politics and Administration', unpublished PhD diss., University of Madras, 1980.

43 Copley, *The Political Career of C. Rajagopalachari*, pp. 288, 295.

44 Aruna Sivakami, 'Rajaji: A Study in Politics and Administration', p. 166.

scheme, and carry on an intense agitation against him. Even if this agitation did not affect the masses much, it had such an impact on a section of the Congress men to build an opposition to Rajaji from within the Congress.

SIGNIFICANCE OF THE EVENTS OF 1953–54

The resignation of Rajaji and the assumption of office by Kamaraj constituted a milestone in the history of Tamil Nadu. Firstly, it marked the 'never-to-return' eclipse of the influence and power of the Brahmin elite in the Congress—the culmination of the process of de-Brahminization begun in 1931 by the increasing participation of the Non-Brahmin community both in the Congress and in the freedom struggle.[45] Secondly, it marked the triumph of democracy within the Congress. A leadership thrown up from among the rank and file during the 1942 Quit India struggle, and maintaining close links with the grassroots, was able to prevail over the central leadership in the choice of chief minister. Thirdly, it may be viewed as the triumph of the party organization over the government. A government which was acting as though it was autonomous of the party had to yield to a government headed by the party president. But this triumph was only momentary. For it resulted in the relegation of the party organization to a secondary role, as the real natural leader of the party became the head of the government, leaving behind shadows to act out the role of party president. A 'K Plan'[46] had to be formulated later to revitalize the party, but by then it was too late. The democratic character of the Congress organization was lost forever, both at the all-India level and at the state level, for similar reasons.

Another significant development was the transformation of

[45] Hardgrave, 'DMK and Politics of Tamil Nationalism'.

[46] K Plan or Kamaraj Plan: a strategy proposed by Kamaraj in 1963 to strengthen the Congress party by senior leaders resigning from government positions to take up party work. Kamaraj himself resigned as chief minister.—*Ed.*

Periyar EVR from an uncompromising extreme anti-Congressism to ardent 'pro-Kamarajism'. Periyar had worked untiringly against the Congress candidates in 1952—the sole exception being made in favour of P. Varadarajulu Naidu; but from now on he stood solidly behind Kamaraj—the first 'true Tamilian' ever to rule the state.[47]

A third development was the end of the radical phase of the DMK and the beginning of the phases of its evolution into a parliamentary Opposition party.[48] The DMK contested the elections in 1957 riding on the popularity gained through its three-pronged movement and the public sympathy the consequent repression had created.

Another significant development was the emergence of caste-based political organizations like the Vanniya Kula Kshatriya Sangam which acted as pressure groups promoting their sectional and caste interests.[49] Thus, Rajaji's education scheme acted unintentionally as a catalytic agent for the generation of diverse forces which were to play significant roles in the politics of Tamil Nadu. The education scheme itself, to which we shall turn again now, having played such an historic role in the drama, made its bow and disappeared into oblivion.

[47] Harrison, *India: The Most Dangerous Decades*, p. 287. Also, R. Parthasarathy, *A Hundred Years of the Hindu*, p. 700.

[48] Barnett, *The Politics of Cultural Nationalism in South India*, p. 79.

[49] Rudolph and Rudolph, 'The Political Role of India's Caste Organisations'. Also, Harrison, *India: The Most Dangerous Decades*, p. 287.

CHAPTER IV

THE CLIMAX AND AFTER

THE PARULEKAR COMMITTEE REPORT (PCR)

The Parulekar Committee consisted exclusively of persons holding the same views as Rajaji. As such, it did not command the respect and attention that an experts' committee was entitled to. Besides, as the *Eastern Economist* pointed out, 'the unanimous report of the committee was unlikely by itself to influence very greatly those whose minds were made up on other grounds'.[1]

The great report, like the great scheme, met the same reception. The *Swatantra* called it a 'pyrrhic victory'.[2] V.R. Krishna Iyer remarked that the Parulekar Committee had damned the scheme with feigned praise.[3] Even C. Subramaniam admitted that the report had not satisfied large sections of the people and said that the government was still examining it.[4]

Educationists were glad that the Parulekar Committee had taken note of the defects in the scheme pointed out by them, and considered the report as a vindication of the stand taken by the South India Teachers' Union (SITU).[5] Pointing out that increased enrolment was not the declared objective of the MSEE as envisaged by the government, the assumption of the Parulekar Committee was questioned on this point.[6] Rajaji had certainly not stated that he had

[1] Editorial, 'Verdict on Rajaji', *Eastern Economist*, vol. 21, October–December 1953. *Viduthalai*, 28 December 1953, published a translation.

[2] *Swatantra*, 5 December 1953.

[3] *Madras Legislative Assembly Debates*, vol. X, 24 December 1953, p. 704.

[4] *Madras Legislative Assembly Debates*, vol. XIII, 26 March 1954, p. 1152.

[5] Editorial, *The South Indian Teacher*, November 1953, p. 447.

[6] Ibid.

introduced the scheme with a view to eradicate illiteracy; nor was he a believer in the necessity for universal elementary education.[7] The anxiety of the Committee that the whole year would pass without increased enrolment unless a special drive was made was itself an admission that the scheme had failed.[8]

The Parulekar Committee's recommendation to pay salaries to young graduates to organize an enrolment drive and to provide funds for training craftsmen and paying them were somewhat naive. 'The state which cannot find the necessary funds for imparting the rudiments of education to all children', 'the state which is unable to increase teachers' salaries' could hardly be expected to find funds for this.[9] Read as a whole, the report left the impression that the scheme as it stood did not fulfil the objectives of speeding up universal elementary education or of making children efficient in crafts. The Committee had recommended additional expenditure on various items such as graduate conscription, paying for craftsmen training, teachers' salaries, etc., little realizing that it was the financial difficulty that had brought about the introduction of the scheme in the first place.[10] The teachers were highly critical of the recommendation of the Committee regarding the increase in pupil–teacher ratio. 'If the government were to stick to the recommendations of the committee, they would have no other way but to dismiss teachers from schools.'[11]

Even though the Education Minister kept assuring the public that the government had not yet made up its mind and was still studying the report, the government began to implement the recommendations. A Curriculum Revision Committee was appointed in December 1953 to follow up on the PCR recommendations to update the curriculum

[7] Srinivasa Iyengar, *Educational India*, June 1954.

[8] Ibid.

[9] Ibid.

[10] Editorial, *Educational India*, January 1954.

[11] T.C. Narayana Nambiar, *Madras Legislative Assembly Debates*, vol. XIII, 26 March 1954, p. 1164. Also, Resolution of Coimbatore Teachers' Guild, *The South Indian Teacher*, December 1953, p. 469.

to suit the 3-hour schooling and out-of-school programme.[12] Government orders were issued extending the scheme to municipal areas.[13] Instructions were issued by the Director of Public Instruction (DPI) to the managers of aided schools to adopt the pupil–teacher ratio recommended by the Parulekar Committee, namely by June 1954, 30:1, by June 1955, 40:1 and by June 1956, 50:1. Schools run by state and local authorities would have a pupil–teacher ratio of 60:1. The surplus teachers were to be utilized for opening new schools or teaching pupils of age group 10–12.[14] A scheme costing Rs 1 crore was evolved to give training to village craftsmen and providing some remuneration to them as an incentive.[15] Undoubtedly, these were preparations to continue the scheme in the academic year 1954–55 with the PCR recommendations incorporated in the scheme. The one recommendation of the PCR about which the government showed little enthusiasm was the increase in teachers' salaries, as it would be tantamount to bribing the teachers to support the scheme.[16] The only incentive was perhaps an amendment whittling down the Madras Educational Rules, which gave wide powers to take action against teachers found unfit or engaging in subversive activities.[17]

Not satisfied with the dubious endorsement of the scheme by the PCR, the government sought further support from the Central Advisory Board of Education (CABE). The CABE considered the scheme at its twenty-first meeting held in February 1954. It was of the opinion that the scheme represented a welcome attempt to bring education within the reach of a large majority of children, and thus helped in the fulfilment of the constitutional directive about providing universal elementary education. The CABE was also satisfied that the

[12] *The South Indian Teacher*, December 1953, p. 475.

[13] *The Hindu*, 3 February 1954.

[14] Ibid.

[15] *Educational India*, March 1954, p. 298.

[16] Resolution of Executive Board of SITU Madras, 13 February 1954. *The South Indian Teacher*, March 1954.

[17] *The South Indian Teacher*, March 1954, p. 25.

reduction of school hours from five to three would not necessarily affect the education of the children adversely, provided that the out-of-school activities—an integral part of the education of children—were implemented under controlled conditions. The CABE further wanted the arrangements made for out-of-school activities to be carefully supervised on the lines suggested by the Parulekar Committee. The scheme was valuable as an interim measure only, because sufficient funds were not available for providing education to all children. The Board was definite that the proper pattern of education for the country was Basic Education which would offer full-time correlated education; teaching of craft as well as of other school subjects would be provided under proper educative conditions in the school itself; and this would serve as a community centre where the school and the community would be brought into an organic relationship. Other states were advised to consider similar experiments under controlled conditions.[18]

This contradicted the statement made by C. Subramaniam on the floor of the Assembly that the CABE had given its endorsement to the principles underlying the MSEE.[19] While the government was propagating that the scheme was unique and ideal for the great educational value it contained—the increase in enrolment being an incidental benefit—the CABE had upheld that full-time schooling alone could offer the education that the children needed. The Madras scheme could be tolerated only as an interim arrangement for increased enrolment. Rajaji had proclaimed that the whole village was a 'polytechnic'. The CABE rejected it by declaring that the school was the true community centre. The CABE had in effect rejected the educational philosophy of Rajaji.

[18] *CABE (1935–1960). Silver Jubilee Souvenir*, p. 299.

[19] *Madras Legislative Assembly Debates*, vol. XIII, 26 March 1954, p. 1151.

WITHDRAWAL OF THE SCHEME

The battle to retain the scheme was thus lost on all fronts. To stick to the scheme would be to jeopardize the Congress in Tamil Nadu. To drop the scheme with Rajaji still in power would be to surrender to the Opposition, causing further damage to the prestige of the Congress government. The only way out was for the architect of the scheme to bow out. Rajaji resigned. Kamaraj took over as chief minister in April 1954. However, C. Subramaniam was retained as education minister.

Almost the first act of the government was to drop the scheme. It was C. Subramaniam's privilege to render the funeral oration for the scheme whose underlying principles were still dear to him and 'whose relevance to time remained unaltered', and for which he had campaigned so seriously all along.[20] The scheme was buried but it was bitter to return to the old system of education which all had rejected. So, a new system was to be evolved as soon as possible that would be consistent with the ultimate pattern of Basic Education. But it would take into consideration the socio-economic needs of a fast-changing society.[21]

The new government appointed an expert committee under the chairmanship of Dr Rm. Alagappa Chettiar.[22] The terms of reference

[20] C. Subramaniam strongly believed that this was a worthwhile scheme. Forty years later, he recalled with some bitterness, that political opponents had 'caricatured Rajaji's scheme'. Periyar wanted 'to use it for a political purpose', 'disgruntled Congress men' joined his agitation, and Kamaraj was not only 'openly speaking against' the scheme but 'the new education scheme came in handy in removing Rajaji from Chief Ministership'. Subramaniam, *Hand of Destiny*, vol. 1, pp. 205–6.—*Ed.*

[21] *Madras Legislative Assembly Debates*, vol. XV, 18 May 1954, pp. 285–91, 452–7.

[22] Rm. Alagappa Chettiar (1909–1957) was an industrialist and philanthropist. Apart from endowing a department of Tamil studies at Travancore University, he established a college at Karaikudi, and played a pivotal role in the founding of the Central Electro Chemical Research Institute (CECRI), Karaikudi, and the A.C. College of Technology, Chennai.—*Ed.*

were to go into the entire system of elementary education, suggest ways and means of implementing the Directive Principles of the Constitution, avoiding wastage, improving the existing system to suit the needs and resources of the state, and converting ordinary schools to Basic schools.[23]

The decision to drop the scheme brought forth an angry response from Rajaji. In a letter to *The Hindu*, he reiterated the virtues of his scheme and his criticism of the existing system of education which was a 'vicious circle of fraud, waste and dreary oppression of children', which caused mass disablement and generated all the bad qualities that went contrary to social cooperation. He regretted that groundless fears of retrenchment, and equally groundless communal apprehensions, and the grievous ignorance of professional politicians in the matter of child psychology had all combined to create an atmosphere wherein no fair trial could be given to a scheme which he prized highly. In his view, it was an experiment on the performance of which the rest of India hoped to benefit from. He asked whether they wanted primary education to be a gamble in which all entrants lost all and gained nothing or training for citizenship.[24] The people of the state should find an answer to this fundamental question, he remarked.

Was this fundamental question answered by the Alagappa Chettiar Committee and by the Kamaraj government? It is to this that we now turn.

[23] G.O. No. 1714, Education, 4 December 1954. The other members of the Committee were: N.D. Sundaravadivelu, Deputy Director of Public Instruction; K. Arunachalam, principal, Teachers' Training College, Sri Ramakrishna Vidyalayam, Periyanaickenpalayam; S. Minakshisundara Mudaliar, Kalaimagal Kalvi Nilayam, Erode; M. Arunachalam, P.K. Nadar's High School, Tirumangalam; and V.S. Gopalakrishna Ayyar, headmaster, Sir M. Ct. Muthiah Chettiar School, Purasawalkam, Madras.

[24] *The Hindu*, 9 June 1954.

THE ALAGAPPA CHETTIAR COMMITTEE REPORT

The Alagappa Chettiar Committee submitted its report in November 1955.[25] The report was not a unanimous one. One member, M. Arunachalam dissented on the question of extending Basic Education.

The Committee, in its report, repeated the old cliché about the harmonious all-round development of the child as the aim of elementary education. Broad and many-sided education, developing to the fullest extent possible the potentialities of the child in the interests of both the individual and the community was needed. Translated in simple words, this meant a return to the status quo prior to June 1953.

The Committee considered five-year schooling to be inadequate. Instead it recommended an integrated education of eight years' duration. It recommended that the six periods a week allotted in higher elementary schools for vocational training should continue. The Committee rejected the reduction of schooling to three hours. Shift system should be resorted to only as a temporary measure wherever the rush for admission was heavy. It suggested that the work programme in Basic schools be made elastic so that children below seven were not strained. It recommended gardening to be introduced as the main craft in place of spinning.

As regards the measures for implementing the Directive Principles of the Constitution, it suggested the following: 1. Establishment of schools in all villages with a population of 300 and above. 2. Provision of free midday meals to schoolchildren subject to the condition that local people share half the cost. 3. Planning of working days such that holidays coincided with seasonal agricultural operations. 4. Continuance of the single-teacher school system, but with only three standards and as a feeder school to normal schools.

The Committee had no worthwhile recommendation to arrest wastage. It believed that midday meals would reduce wastage. It also

[25] *Report of the Elementary Education Reform Committee, Madras State, 1955* (hereafter *REERC*).

did not suggest any significant change in the curriculum, except incorporation of features of Basic schools. In short, the Committee appeared to believe that the existing (pre-1953) school system did not require any drastic change as advocated by Rajaji. The goals of universal education as well as the socialization of the child could be achieved within the framework of the existing system. However, the Committee did recommend better emoluments for the teachers.

EDUCATION UNDER THE KAMARAJ GOVERNMENT

Were the assumptions on which the MSEE was based valid and do they have relevance today? Or were the obstacles in the way of rapid spread of education overcome or could be overcome by a varied approach? The Kamaraj Era is here taken up for a brief comparative analysis to answer these questions.

Accepting the recommendations of the Alagappa Chettiar Committee, the Kamaraj government gave top priority to the spread of elementary education. The government had already initiated measures to provide educational facilities to all the villages in the state with a population of not less than 500 before the end of 1955–56. Local bodies were directed to concentrate on the provision of facilities for elementary education until an adequate number of elementary education schools were established. Expansion of facilities for secondary education was deferred. Availing of the financial aid given by the Government of India for the relief of the 'Educated Unemployed' under the First Five-Year Plan, single teacher schools were opened, while the existing schools were strengthened with additional teachers. As many as 4,267 elementary schools were opened during the Plan period. All villages with a population of 300 and above were provided with schools and more than four lakhs of children were additionally enrolled in them. Thus, the method chosen for the spread of elementary education was mainly the expansion of school facilities. Between 1956–57 and 1971–72, the number of schools increased from 25,268 to 32,021, and the number of pupils from 30.88 lakhs to 65.77 lakhs.[26]

Another measure to increase enrolment without increasing cost was to adopt the recommendation of the Parulekar Committee regarding the pupil–teacher ratio. The ratio was increased to 35:1 with effect from 1958,[27] 40:1 from 1961[28] and 45:1 from 1963.[29] The objective was to double the pupil-turnout–population ratio from 10 per 1,000 to 20 per 1,000, while reducing the cost of education per pupil from Rs 200 to Rs 150 by 1965–66.[30]

The shift system adopted under the regime of Omandur P. Ramaswamy Reddiar was revived wherever there was demand for increased admission. A scheme of compulsory education was introduced from 1960–61, in a phased programme spread over three years. Every child between 6 and 7 years of age was compulsorily enrolled in school. No child was allowed to withdraw before reaching the fifth standard or attaining 12 years of age, whichever was earlier. As a result of this measure, more than three lakh children were additionally enrolled, and about 6,600 more teachers employed.[31]

To overcome the socio-economic hurdles, a number of measures were taken. Elementary education was made free for all poor children, irrespective of caste or community. Fee concession was withdrawn only if the pupil failed to pass even at the second attempt.[32] (Earlier, it was withdrawn if the pupil failed even once.[33])

The most spectacular measure was the midday meals scheme.

[26] *Perspective Plan for Tamil Nadu: Towards a Learning Society*, p. 1.

[27] G.O. No. 639, Education, 2 April 1958.

[28] G.O. No. 211, Education, 25 January 1961.

[29] G.O. No. 1974, Education, 4 September 1963.

[30] Lalithalakshmi, 'Kamaraj as Administrator', PhD diss., University of Madras, 1981.

[31] Ibid. Quoting G.O. No. 637, Education, 28 March 1959; G.O. No. 635, Education & Public Health, 2 April 1963.

[32] Ibid. Quoting G.O. No. 1100, Education, 5 June 1956.

[33] Ibid. Quoting G.O. No. 926, Education, 19 May 1955.

This scheme was already in vogue in the Harijan Welfare Schools and Madras Corporation schools. It was first tried in 1945 in selected areas where the Compulsory Education Act was in force but had been suspended in 1947 in the face of acute financial stringency.[34] Kamaraj revived the scheme and placed it on a regular footing by subsidizing the costs as a part of the Education Plan on a 60:40 basis—60 per cent being the state's share while the rest was covered by local public voluntary contribution. By 1962, an overwhelming 26,406 schools out of 27,135 were covered by the scheme. Eleven lakh eighty thousand pupils were benefited at a cost of Rs 115 lakhs.[35] In addition to the

[34] G.O. No. 386, Education, 8 March 1947. This government order was in pursuance of the Government of India directive of 31 July 1946 that provincial governments re-examine their plan with a view to reducing the expenditure, in particular on education, and increasing allotment on agriculture and health. The file on increasing allotment makes for interesting reading, as the following extract shows: 'Improvement in food position will mean improvement in the quantity available under ration cards of individual families. So it may be unnecessary to continue to offer inducement through free midday meals. If even after improvement of food position, attendance at schools is not regular, penal provisions in Compulsory Education Act may have to be resorted to.'

[In 1945 the government drew up a postwar plan to introduce compulsory elementary education all over the state. The implementation began immediately in rural areas, and in three years it had been implemented in 1,831 centres. Prakasam, as premier during 1946–47, wanted to convert all primary schools to Basic schools. But it proved to be a costly affair as the cotton for spinning was wasted in many cases. Because of the costs many schools were closed down (Subramaniam, *Hand of Destiny*, vol. 1, p. 204). Expansion was suspended in 1948–49, pending review. But the primary reason was the decision to introduce Basic Education throughout the state at the earliest. Although the government swore by 'universal, free and compulsory elementary education . . . in the shortest time possible', 'the heavy expenditure involved and the difficulties in obtaining the army of teachers required . . . and the very large number of buildings necessary for housing the new schools proved to be deterrents.' As of March 1952, therefore, the scheme was in operation in only 30 of the 97 municipalities in Madras State. G.O. No. 816, Education, 9 April 1952.—*Ed.*]

[35] Lalithalakshmi, 'Kamaraj as Administrator'.

midday meals scheme, the School Improvement Scheme was launched all over the state, by which local people were involved voluntarily in the development of school facilities and in providing books, slates, uniforms, etc. for poor children.[36]

Realizing that contented teachers were the guarantee for the success of any educational effort, a series of measures to improve their service conditions were taken: better provident fund benefits, increased pay and dearness allowance, free education up to SSLC for children of elementary school teachers, loan scholarships to children of teachers for post-matric professional education, state awards for outstanding teachers, etc.[37]

The above brief, if rosy, survey may evoke certain questions: What was the additional expenditure incurred to obtain the increase in enrolment? Was it higher or lower than that estimated by the framers of the MSEE? Was the wastage withdrawal from the school before completing five years of education reduced by the above measures to overcome socio-economic factors? Was there any significant improvement in the standard of living of the poor that they voluntarily forewent the labour of their children? Was there really a miracle? Were all the fears of Parulekar, Naik and the Rajaji government that full enrolment could not be ensured unless expenditure on education, number of schools and teachers were doubled, justified?

To answer these questions, we should bear in mind that the advance in education made during the Kamaraj era was not an isolated phenomenon peculiar to Tamil Nadu; it was an integral part of the advance made by India as a whole during the first three Plan periods. But for the Plan's general policy and allocation of funds, the state government could not have made headway. The credit lies in the committed and vigorous application of the national policy by the Kamaraj government.

The correlation between the increase in enrolment and the

36 Ibid.

37 'Benefits for the Teachers', *Madras Information*, September 1962.

increase in number of schools, number of teachers and the annual expenditure on elementary education has been analysed by many educationists and administrators, both at the all-India level and at the state level.[38]

Table 4.1 furnishes the particulars of enrolment in elementary schools and expenditure on elementary education in India as a whole for 1955–56 and 1965–66. Table 4.2 furnishes similar data in respect of Tamil Nadu for 1956 and 1962.

The two tables reveal that the expenditure on elementary education had increased at a faster rate than the enrolment in primary schools. If we take into account the fact of higher pupil–teacher ratios and the shift systems during this period, it is clear that if one hundred per cent enrolment is to be achieved, the outlay on elementary education would have to be of a higher order.

It should also be noted that the enrolment data does not reveal the state of affairs fully. Firstly, enrolment figures tend to be exaggerated for various reasons. Secondly, all that they indicate is that the pupils were enrolled, and not that all the enrolled students indeed attended school.

Statistics regarding dropouts and wastage are more revealing. As of August 1974, the number of pupils studying in Class V were 5.27 lakhs as against 10.05 lakhs studying in Class I.[39] The Research Bureau of Teachers' College, Madras, undertook a study of wastage and stagnation and made an analysis of the career of 1,191 pupils in 51 schools, beginning in 1956–57. It was found that of the 1,191 pupils, only 124 completed Class V in 5 years; 334 dropped out after

38 The analysis below draws on the following: *Perspective Plan for Tamil Nadu: Towards a Learning Society*; Goel, *Education and Economic Growth in India*; Saini, *Development of Education in India*; Adiseshiah et al. (eds), *Backdrop to the Learning Society*; Venkatasubramanian, *Education and Economic Development in India*; University of Delhi, Agricultural Economics Research Centre, *Primary Education in Rural India: Participation and Wastage.*

39 Joshua, *Rural Primary Education and Adult Literacy in Tamil Nadu*, p. 33 (Table 10).

TABLE 4.1

Enrolment in Primary Schools and Expenditure on Elementary School Education in India

S. No Col.1	*Item* Col. 2	*1955–56* Col. 3	*1965–66* Col. 4	*Ratio* Col. 4/Col. 3
1	Enrolment in Class I–V (millions)	25.1 (52.8)	50.5 (76.7)	2.0 (1.5)
2	Enrolment in Class VI–VIII (millions)	4.3 (16.5)	10.5 (30.8)	2.5 (1.8)
3	Total Expenditure on Education (in Rs crores)	190	622	
4	Expenditure on Elementary Education			
	(i) As percent of (3) above	56	30	
	(ii) In Rs Crores	106	186	1.8

Note:
(1) Figures in brackets indicate percentages of age-cohorts.
(2) Line 4 (i): The percentages pertain to the outlays of First and Third Five-Year Plans.
(3) Line 4 (ii): 3 multiplied by 4 (i).

Source:
S.K. Saini, *Development of Education in India*, Tables 8.1 and 8.2.

Class I, 231 after Class II, 190 after Class III and 175 after Class IV. Thus 930 pupils out of 1,191 investigated did not reach Class V.[40]

An analysis by the State Planning Commission shows that only 4.22 lakhs out of the 8.74 lakhs enrolled in 1957–58 in Class I reached

[40] Ibid., pp. 46–7.

TABLE 4.2

Enrolment in Primary Schools and Expenditure on Elementary Education in Tamil Nadu

S. No	*Item*	*1956*	*1962*	*Ratio*
Col. 1	Col. 2	Col. 3	Col. 4	Col. 4/Col. 3
1	Enrolment in primary schools (millions)	2.9 (56)	4.0 (60)	1.34 (1.07)
2	Total expenditure on education (in Rs crores)	109.5	187.2	1.7
3	Expenditure on elementary Education			
	(i) As percentage of (2)	80	72	
	(ii) in Rs crores	87.5	135	1.54

Note:

(1) Figures in brackets indicate percentages of age-cohorts.

(2) 3 (i) Percentage of expenditure on elementary education in First and Second Five-Year Plans as given in *Perspective Plan for Tamil Nadu: Towards a Learning Society*.

(3) 3 (ii): (2) multiplied by 3 (i).

Source:

(1) Particulars of enrolment (1962) and total expenditure (1956 and 1962), taken from Lalithalakshmi, 'Kamaraj as Administrator'.

(2) Enrolment for 1956 taken from the Madras Administration Report.

Class V by 1961–62. More than fifty per cent failed to complete lower primary education.[41]

According to the Education Commission (1964–66), 65 per cent of the wastage was due to poverty.[42] The Task Force of the Tamil Nadu

[41] *Perspective Plan for Tamil Nadu: Towards a Learning Society*, p. 7; the Education Commission 1964–66 also confirms this wastage.

[42] Quoted in Joshua, *Rural Primary Education and Adult Literacy in*

State Planning Commission also reported that there seemed to be a curious relation between the 51.2 per cent wastage in the first four standards and 40 per cent of the people in rural areas and 60 per cent of the people in the urban areas living below the poverty line.[43]

A study undertaken by the Agricultural Economics Research Cell of the University of Delhi under Amartya Sen's chairmanship in 1967 came to the same conclusion.

> External factors like income and caste are more relevant in explaining internal factors affecting quality of education. One internal factor, namely the timing of rural primary school, seemed to have considerable bearing on the question of wastage at primary school. Complete lack of synchronization between agricultural seasonality and school timing led to a sharp fall in attendance during agricultural peak seasons. Children worked with their parents in the family farm or even found jobs on a contractual basis. Educational backwardness is largely a symptom of economic backwardness.[44]

Amartya Sen further remarked that

> Research directed towards formulating school curriculum which will involve shorter school hours and allow for its variation over the years in accordance with the intensity of agricultural activity

Tamil Nadu, p. 60.

[43] *Perspective Plan for Tamil Nadu: Towards a Learning Society*, p. 9. The figures relating to population below poverty line seem to require correction. Applying the criterion of 2,400 calories per person per day, 46 per cent in rural areas and 37 per cent in urban areas are below poverty line. M. Ramamurthy has estimated that 73.80 per cent of the rural population earn less than Rs 38.75 per month at 1969–70 prices, considered the minimal living income. Joshua, *Rural Primary Education and Adult Literacy in Tamil Nadu*, p. 15.

[44] *Primary Education in Rural India: Participation and Wastage*, p. 77.

is likely to be a highly worthwhile area of investigation.[45]

Such solutions, however, are only partial—without eliminating the fundamental problems of economic and social backwardness, no satisfactory solution can be possible.[46] The wastage is that of the state resources diverted for education. The state increased its expenditure on education from Rs 15 crores in 1961 to Rs 89 crores in 1972 entailing a rate of increase of nearly fifty per cent per annum, while the net State Domestic Product increased at a compound rate of only 3.5 per cent over the same period.[47] At this rate of increase, remarked Malcolm Adiseshiah, by the end of the Seventh Plan, education will use up the entire annual budget of the state.[48]

As C.T. Kurien points out, '[T]he phenomenal increase in educational expenditure by "society" has gone primarily to providing an education or miseducation for a few who are the affluent, influential and powerful while the vast majority of the people have gone away empty handed.'[49] All attempts to find a solution to the problem of achieving one hundred per cent literacy, of avoiding wastage in primary education within the framework of the existing socio-economic system, finally lead us to one form or other of the Rajaji Scheme.[50] The Non-Formal System of Education publicized from the late 1970s as the magic wand for achieving total literacy is an admission that under the present system, dropouts or 'push-outs' are inevitable and the only solution is to bring those poor pupils pushed out to child labour back to a brief hour of schooling after their working hours; a sort of inverted Rajaji Scheme, or worse, Vinoba's. So, it was back to square one after three decades.

[45] Ibid.

[46] Ibid.

[47] *Perspective Plan for Tamil Nadu: Towards a Learning Society*, p. 14.

[48] Adiseshiah, 'Launching of Non-Formal Education in Tamil Nadu', p. 22.

[49] Adiseshiah et al. (eds), *Backdrop to the Learning Society*, p. 29.

[50] Ibid., pp. 72, 138, 238, 358.

RELEVANCE OF THE SCHEME TO FUTURE SOCIO-ECONOMIC DEVELOPMENT

We have thus far considered how the socio-economic conditions of the people have adversely affected and continue to affect the progress of universalization of primary education, and how some variant or other of the Parulekar–Naik–Rajaji model—such as the part-time education for school dropouts contemplated under the non-formal education programmes—could alone be thought of if one had to work within the existing socio-economic-political system. We shall now examine whether the Rajaji model can be adapted as an agent of socio-economic-political change and development, and if so to what extent.

We discussed earlier how the Gandhian Basic Education Scheme and the Rajaji variant of it were envisaged to serve a self-reliant, self-sufficient, self-contented rural economy in a highly de-centralized, de-bureaucratized socio-political setup in which human needs would be few and most simple.[51] Gandhi's process of socialization of the child takes place within the school where the child learns all about the world through the craft of the community in which it lives. In Rajaji's scheme, the education in subjects is separated from the socialization process which takes place outside the school, in the work activity of the village, with the child participating in the activity directly. It is assumed that the idyllic community of Gandhi's vision exists in the villages.

But the nation under the leadership of Jawaharlal Nehru had taken a different path. A modern industrial economy was being built up with heavy industry as the core. The modernization process was extended to the villages. Community development projects and agricultural extension schemes had as their aim the adaptation of advanced extension techniques, as conceived and applied in the West, to local conditions and resources of Indian villages and the transformation of

[51] Mukherjee, *Gandhi: A Study*, p. 216.

the social and economic life of the village.[52] The Nehruvian strategy consisted of a centrally-planned economy developed according to a series of Five-Year Plans, which involved a vast bureaucracy to ensure their execution. The incongruence of the Gandhian Basic Education model in such a set-up was realized by Gandhi himself, when he said that if people thought machines to be really indispensable, they should reject his scheme and suggest a new one.[53]

When Gandhi's scheme, in which craft and education are closely interlinked, and the dualism between manual and intellectual labour is itself found incompatible with the path of socio-economic development the nation has chosen, the more incompatible was Rajaji's scheme in which craft and education are delinked, with the intellectual skills being taken care of by the school and manual skills by the community which itself is riven into labouring and exploiting classes. Rajaji's scheme was therefore not relevant to socio-economic development.

Attempts to modify Basic Education to suit changing social needs by adding other productive activities like engineering, electronics, etc., too failed. As M. Arunachalam in his dissent note pointed out, most crafts have 'limited scope for affording educational possibilities for correlation'. Failing to solve the problem of correlation, attempts were made to graft certain features of Basic Education to a non-Basic system of primary education and make the non-Basic schools 'Basic-oriented' by introducing simple crafts and activities like social service, community living, cultural and recreational programmes.[54]

52 Thirumalai, 'Post War Agricultural Problems and Policies in India' (1954), in *Rural Sociology in India*, ed. A.R. Desai, p. 537.

53 Quoted by M. Arunachalam in his dissent note to the Elementary Education Reform Committee, Madras State, 1955, *REERC*, p. 52. Arunachalam wanted the claims of Basic Education to be examined critically in light of the nation having thrown in its lot with industrialization. Pointing out that almost all Basic Schools had fallen into the same old rut as traditional primary schools, he averred that all attempts to graft various crafts for correlating to educational needs had failed.

54 *Third Five-Year Plan*, p. 582.

The question arises whether any such 'orientation' of schools to the Rajaji pattern is possible. The only distinguishing feature of the Rajaji scheme, so far as the educational philosophy was concerned, was the out-of-school activity—children participating in the work of their parents or village artisans. To incorporate this feature in normal schools would be to adopt the Rajaji scheme as such, which, as already noted, was not compatible with the national objectives of economic development. Excursions, weekend and seasonal participation in field work and similar activities were not adequate to create the spirit behind Rajaji's scheme that sought total identification of the child with the community in which he lived. Only in a classless society would it be possible to have a proper system of education that would unite thinking and doing in the form of productive work, and end the dualism between intellectual and manual labour and the hiatus between the school and the community.

CONCLUSION

From the foregoing narrative and analysis of the Modified Scheme of Elementary Education (MSEE), certain features may be recognized and broad conclusions drawn—firstly, in regard to the political developments, and then in regard to the educational aspects of the controversy. The group conflict within the Congress, the broad democratic aspirations of Telugu sub-nationalism, the emergence of a strong Non-Brahmin movement with considerable influence upon the Congress, the emergence of the Communist movement, all combined to make the political spectrum complex. The bad showing of the Congress in the 1952 elections brought Rajaji back into Tamil Nadu politics from his self-imposed retirement. The opportunistic and undemocratic methods employed by him to instal a Congress government in the state did not augur well for an infant democracy. Rajaji's stubborn refusal to gracefully accept the resolution of the legislature on the scheme and the way he was eased out of office by a rival faction did much harm to the healthy growth of parliamentary democracy.

Despite the striking progress that education had recorded during the first few years after Independence, the implementation of the constitutional directive under Article 45 of the Constitution remained a distant dream. As a Gandhian, Rajaji had his own ideological reservations about the desirability of institutionalized education. This, coupled with the obligation to honour the constitutional directive, led him to the formulation and implementation of the MSEE. A comparative study of the developments in the field of education in the West reveals that educational expansion is inseparably linked with industrial revolution; the movement for universal compulsory education was triggered by the economic changes inextricably associated with the movement of the working classes for their rights, especially those regarding working hours and employment of children. Thus, the politicization of education was inevitable.

However, the politicization of the MSEE falls into an altogether different category. It was not so much the reservations of the educationists about its postulates, not even the irrelevance of its socio-economic philosophy (essentially Gandhian in the context of the nation opting for the capitalist path of development), but the violation of principles of political democracy in its ushering in that brought about its immediate politicization. The undemocratic manner in which the scheme was introduced, overruling the objections raised by the Education Department, the disrespect to the legislature by disregarding its resolution—all these helped the forces hostile to Rajaji both within the Congress and those outside to exploit the fears that it had aroused in the minds of the underprivileged, and foredoomed it to failure.

But the scheme was not substituted by any revolutionary measure suited to the needs of the nation. Despite the spectacular expansion in elementary education under the Kamaraj regime, a high level of wastage and stagnation continued and nullified all efforts for mass literacy. For these were caused by social inequalities and dire poverty of the vast majority of the people. Hence, the state had to revert to an inverted form of the Rajaji scheme under the cloak of non-formal education, working within the framework of the existing socio-economic system. A quarter century of this dual system of education, wherein the poor and the underprivileged were served with an inferior kind of education by schools run by government and local bodies free of charge in the mother tongue of the children, while a small minority of the rich and the privileged elite classes have the benefit of a superior kind of education through private English medium schools, has brought about a situation in which the children of the poor drop out of school even before they have learnt anything.

BIBLIOGRAPHY

UNPUBLISHED RECORDS

Tamil Nadu Archives

Proceedings of the Education Department of the Government of Madras, 1952–54

Tamil Nadu Congress Committee, Madras

Minutes of the meetings of Executive Committee, 1955

GOVERNMENT OF MADRAS (TAMIL NADU) PUBLICATIONS

Madras Legislative Assembly Debates, 1952–54

Madras Legislative Council Debates, 1953–54

Madras State Administration Reports (Annual), 1945–46 to 1954–55

Perspective Plan for Tamil Nadu: Towards a Learning Society: A Plan for Education, Science and Technology, 1972–1984. Madras: State Planning Commission, 1972.

Progress of Education in Madras State. Madras, 1954.

Report of the Committee on Elementary Education in Madras, 1953. Madras: Director of Information and Publicity, Government of Madras, 1953.

Report of the Elementary Education Reform Committee, Madras State, 1955. Madras: Superintendent, Government Press, 1955.

Report on Public Instruction in the Madras State for the Year 1952–53. Madras: Superintendent, Government Press, 1957.

GOVERNMENT OF INDIA

Indian Educational Documents Since Independence: Committees, Commissions, Conferences. Edited by Arabinda Biswas and Suresh Agarwal. New Delhi: Academic Publishers, 1971.

Central Advisory Board of Education. *CABE (1935–1960). Silver Jubilee Souvenir*. Delhi: Government of India, 1960.

Third Five Year Plan, 1961–66. Delhi: Government of India.

BOOKS AND ARTICLES IN ENGLISH

Adiseshiah, Malcolm, ed. *Backdrop to the Learning Society: Education Perspective for Tamilnadu*. Madras: Madras Institute of Development Studies, 1978.

———. 'Launching of Non-Formal Education in Tamil Nadu'. *MIDS Bulletin*, vol. V, no. 5 & 6 (May–June 1975), pp. 320–6.

Ahluwalia, B.K., and S. Ahluwalia. *Rajaji and Gandhi*. New Delhi: Allora Publishers, 1978.

Ahmad, Karuna. 'Towards a Study of Education and Social Change'. *Economic & Political Weekly*, vol. 14, no. 4 (27 January 1979).

Arnold, David. *The Congress in Tamilnad: Nationalist Politics in South India, 1919–1937*. Delhi: Manohar Publishers, 1977.

Baker, C.J., and David Washbrook. *South India: Political Institutions and Political Change, 1880–1940*. Delhi: Macmillan Publishers, 1975.

Baker, C.J. *Politics of South India, 1920–1937*. Delhi: Cambridge University Press, 1976.

Barnett, Marguerite Ross. *The Politics of Cultural Nationalism in South India*. Princeton: Princeton University Press, 1976.

Beteille, Andre. *Caste, Class and Power*. Berkeley: University of California Press, 1965.

Blaug, Mark. *An Introduction to the Economics of Education*. Harmondsworth: Penguin, 1976.

Brembeck, Cole S. *Social Foundations of Education: Environmental Influences in Teaching and Learning*. New York: John Wiley & Sons, 1966.

Chaudhuri, Pramit. *The Indian Economy: Poverty and Development*. Delhi: Vikas Publishing House, 1979.

Chockalingam, T.S. *Kamaraj*. Madras: Navayuga Prachuralayam, 1955.

Colletti, Lucio. *From Rousseau to Lenin*. Bombay: Oxford University Press, 1978.

Copley, Antony R.H. *The Political Career of C. Rajagopalachari, 1937–1954: A Moralist in Politics*. Delhi: Macmillan Publishers, 1978.

Curle, Adam. *Educational Strategy for Developing Societies*. London: Tavistock Publications, 1963.

Desai, A.R. *Social Background of Indian Nationalism*. Bombay: Popular Prakashan, 1976.

———. *Rural Sociology in India*. Bombay: Indian Society of Agricultural Economics (ISAE), 1961.

Desai, D.M. *Compulsory Education in India*. Pune: Indian Institute of Education, 1953.

Kumar, Dharma. *Land and Caste in South India*. Cambridge: Cambridge University Press, 1965.

Du Bois, W.E.B. *The Education of Black People*. New York: Monthly Review Press, 1973.

Dupuis, A.M. *Philosophy of Education in Historical Perspective*. Chicago: Thomson Press, 1972.

Dutt, Rajani Palme. *India Today*. Calcutta: Manisha Granthalaya, 1979.

Dutt, Vishnu. *Gandhi, Nehru and the Challenge*. New Delhi: Abhinav Publishers, 1975.

Erdman, Howard L. *The Swatantara Party and Indian Conservatism*. Cambridge: Cambridge University Press, 1967.

Gandhi, M.K. *Educational Reconstruction*. Wardha: Hindustani Talimi Sangh, 1950.

———. *Basic Education*. Edited by B. Kumarappa. Ahmedabad: Navajivan Press, 1951.

———. *Economic and Industrial Life and Revolution*. Edited by V.B. Kher. 2 vols. Ahmedabad: Navajivan Press, 1968.

———. *Selected Works*. Vol. III, *The Basic Works*, edited by Shriman Narayan. Ahmedabad: Navajivan Press, 1968.

Gandhi, Rajmohan. *The Rajaji Story*. Vol. I, *A Warrior from the South*. Madras: Bharathan Publications, 1973.

Ganguli, B.N. *Gandhi's Social Philosophy: Perspective and Relevance*. Delhi: Vikas Publishing House, 1973.

Goel, S.C. *Education and Economic Growth in India*. Delhi: Macmillan Publishers, 1975.

Gopalakrishnan, P.K. *Development of Economic Ideas in India*. Delhi: People's Publishing House, 1959.

Gordon, D.S. *Principles and Practice of Education*. Mysore: Christian Literature Society, 1957.

Hardgrave, Robert L. 'DMK and Politics of Tamil Nationalism'. *Pacific Affairs*, vol. 37, no. 4, 1964.

———. *Nadars of Tamilnad: The Political Culture of a Community in Change*. Bombay: Oxford University Press, 1969.

Harrison, S. Selig. *India: The Most Dangerous Decades*. Madras: Oxford University Press, 1968.

Heimsath, C.H. *Indian Nationalism and Hindu Social Reform*. Princeton: Princeton University Press, 1964.

Illich, Ivan. *Deschooling Society*. New York: Harper & Row, 1972.

Irschick, Eugene F. 'Significance of Justice Party'. In *Justice Party Golden Jubilee Souvenir*. Madras: 1968.

———. *Politics and Social Conflict in South India: The Non-Brahman Movement and Tamil Separatism, 1916–1929*. Bombay: Oxford University Press, 1969.

John, V.V. *The Great Classroom Hoax & Other Reflections on India's Education*. Delhi: Vikas Publishing House, 1978.

Joshua, Alexander. *Rural Primary Education and Adult Literacy in Tamil Nadu*. Madras: Madras Institute of Development Studies, 1978.

Kabir, Humayun. *Indian Philosophy of Education*. Bombay: Asia Publishing House, 1961.

Kashyap, Subhash C. *Indian Political Parties: Programmes, Promises and Performance*. Delhi: Research Publications in Social Science, 1971.

Krelis, George S. *The Individual and his Education*. Arlington: American

Vocational Association, 1972.
Kripalani, J.B. *The Latest Fad, Basic Education*. Wardha: Hindustani Talimi Sangh, 1946.
Kumarappa, J.C. *Economy of Permanence*. Delhi: Akhil Bharat Sarva Seva Sangh, 1971.
Kuppuswamy, B. *Social Change in India*. Delhi: Vikas Publishing House, 1972.
Lieten, G.K. 'Caste in Class Politics'. *Economic & Political Weekly*, vol. 14, nos. 7 & 8 (Annual Number, February 1979).
Madan, T.N. 'Social Organisation'. In *Economic History of India*, edited by V.B. Singh. Delhi: Allied Publishers, 1965.
Majumdar, R.C., ed. *The History and Culture of Indian People*. Volume XI, *The Struggle for Freedom*. Bombay: Bharatiya Vidya Bhavan, 1978.
Mangalamurugesan, N.K. *Self-Respect Movement in Tamil Nadu, 1920–1940*. Madurai: Koodal Publishers, 1980.
Mani, R.S. *Educational Ideals of Gandhi and Tagore*. Delhi: New Book Society of India, 1961.
Marx, Karl. *Critique of the Gotha Programme*. Moscow: Progress Publishers, 1980.
Menon, Gopala. 'Non-Brahmin Movement and Justice Party'. In *Justice Party Golden Jubilee Souvenir*. Madras: 1968.
Mukherjee, Hiren. *Gandhi: A Study*. 1960. Rev. ed. Delhi: People's Publishing House, 1979.
———. *India Struggles for Freedom: A History*. Bombay: Kutub Publishers, 1948.
———. *The Gentle Colossus: A Study of Jawaharlal Nehru*. Delhi: Jaico Publishing House, 1969.
Mukherjee, K.C. *Underdevelopment, Educational Policy and Planning*. Bombay: Asia Publishing House, 1967.
Mundasseri, Joseph. 'Modern Educational Reforms'. *New Age*, February 1956.
Myrdal, Gunnar. *Asian Drama: An Inquiry into the Poverty of Nations*. 3 vols. Harmondsworth: Penguin, 1968.
Naik, J.P. *Elementary Education in India: The Unfinished Business*. Bombay: Asia Publishing House, 1966.
Nair, T.M. 'Political Reconstruction in India'. In *Justice Party Golden Jubilee Souvenir*. Madras: 1968.
Nambiar, S.R. 'Meaning of Basic Education'. *New Age*, September 1965.
Namboodiripad, E.M.S. 'Caste Conflicts vs Growing Unity of Popular Democratic Forces'. *Economic & Political Weekly*, vol. 14, nos. 7 & 8 (Annual Number, February 1979).
———. *The Mahatma and the Ism*. Delhi: People's Publishing House, 1958.
Narasimhachari, K.T. *C. Rajagopalachari: His Life and Mind*. Delhi: B.R. Chawla, Heritage Publishers, 1978.
Narasimhan, V.K. *Kamaraj: A Study*. Bombay: Manaktalas Publishers, 1967.

Nehru, Jawaharlal. *An Autobiography*. London: Bodley Head, 1947.

Ojha, Pandit G.K. *Progress of Compulsory Education in India, 1951–56*. Delhi: Universal Book and Stationary India, 1966.

Pandhe, M.L., ed. *Child Labour in India*. Calcutta: India Book Exchange, 1979.

Parker, S.C. *The History of Modern Elementary Education*. Boston: Ginn and Co, 1912.

Parthasarathy, R. *A Hundred Years of the Hindu: The Epic Story of Indian Nationalism*. Madras: Kasturi & Sons, 1980.

Parulekar, R.V. *Shri R.V. Parulekar Felicitation Volume*. Bombay: A.N. Samant, for the R.V. Parulekar 71st Birthday Celebration Committee, 1956.

Patel, Vallabhbhai. *Correspondence*. Volume II, *Elections to Central & Provincial Legislatures: Direction of Congress Campaign*, edited by Durga Das. Ahmedabad: Navajivan Press, 1972.

Perumal, Nilkan. *Rajaji: A Biographical Study*. Calcutta: Maya Publications, 1948.

Pillai, K.K. *Caste System in Tamil Nadu*. Madras: University of Madras, 1977.

Rajagopalachari, C. *Chats Behind Bars*. Madras: S. Ganesan, 1931.

———. *Ambedkar Refuted*. Bombay: Hind Kitab, 1946.

———. *Jail Diary*. Madras: Rochouse & Sons, 1921.

———. *Satyam Eva Jayate: A Collection of Articles Contributed to* Swarajya *and Other Journals from 1956 to 1961*. Madras: Bharathan Publications, 1961.

———. *Speeches*. 2 vols. Bombay: Bharatiya Vidya Bhavan, 1958.

———. *Speeches Delivered as Governor of West Bengal, 15 April 1944 -14 June 1948*. Government of West Bengal.

Ram, N. 'Dravidian Movement in its Pre-Independence Phase'. *Economic & Political Weekly*, vol. 14, nos. 7 & 8 (Annual Number, February 1979).

Ramanathan, G. *Education from Dewey to Gandhi: The Theory of Basic Education*. Bombay: Asia Publishing House, 1962.

Rao, G.R. *Progressive Madras State: A Saga of Integrated Development*. Madras: Hindustan Chamber of Commerce, 1967.

Ray, Sibnarayan, ed. *Gandhi, India and the World: An International Symposium*. Philadelphia: Temple University Press, 1970.

Rudolph, Lloyd, and Susan Rudolph. 'The Political Role of India's Caste Organisations'. *Pacific Affairs*, vol. 33, no. 1 (March 1960).

Ruthnasamy, M. 'Justice Party as I Knew It'. In *Justice Party Golden Jubilee Souvenir*. Madras: 1968.

Saini, S.K. *Development of Education in India*. Delhi: Cosmo Publications, 1980.

Saiyidain, K.G., J.P. Naik, and S. Abid Husain. *Compulsory Education in India*. Paris: UNESCO, 1952. Reprint, Delhi: Universal Book and Stationary Co., 1966. Page references are to the 1966 edition.

Sampath, P.N. 'CR's Leadership in Retrospect'. *Swatantra*, 10 April 1954.

Saraswathi, S. 'The Justice Party, 1916–20'. In *Justice Party Golden Jubilee*

Souvenir. Madras: 1968.

Sen, N.B. *Glorious Thoughts of Nehru*. Delhi: New Book Society of India, 1964.

Sharma, S.R. 'Cottage Industries'. In *Economic History of India, 1857–1956*, edited by V.B. Singh. Bombay: Allied Publishers, 1965.

Narayan, Shriman. *Towards the Gandhian Plan*. Delhi: S. Chand & Co, 1978.

Sidhartha, Ranjani. 'Education'. In *Economic History of India, 1857–1956*, edited by V.B. Singh. Bombay: Allied Publishers, 1965.

Simon, Brian. *Studies in the History of Education, 1780–1870: Education and the Labour Movement*. London: Lawrence and Wishart, 1960.

Singh, V.B. 'Village Community'. In *Economic History of India, 1857–1956*, edited by Singh. Bombay: Allied Publishers, 1965.

———, ed. *Economic History of India, 1857–1956*. Bombay: Allied Publishers, 1965.

Srinivas, M.N. *Caste in India*. Bombay: Asia Publishing House, 1962.

———. *Social Change in Modern India*. Bombay: Allied Publishers, 1966.

Srinivasa Iyengar, R. *On Education and Educationists*. Madras: Printed by author, 1957.

Subbaraman, P.S. *Kamaraj: Symbol of Indian Democracy*. Bombay: Popular Prakashan, 1966.

Subramaniam, T.V. 'The Tamil Brahmins: Some Guidelines to Research on their Emergence and Eclipse'. *Economic & Political Weekly*, vol. 4, July 1969.

Thirumalai, S. 'Post War Agricultural Problems and Policies in India'. In *Rural Sociology in India*, edited by A.R. Desai. Bombay: Indian Society of Agricultural Economics, 1961.

Turchenko, V. *Scientific and Technological Revolution and Revolution in Education*. Moscow: Progress Publishers, 1976.

UNESCO. *Learning to be* (abridged). Delhi: NCERT, 1974.

———. *Regional Seminar on Alternative Approaches to School Education at Primary Level, Manila, 6–14 December 1976*. UNESCO, 1977.

University of Delhi, Agricultural Economics Research Centre. *Primary Education in Rural India: Participation and Wastage*. Delhi: Tata-McGraw Hill, 1971.

Venkatasubramanian, K. *Education and Economic Development in India*. Delhi: Frank Bros. & Co., 1980.

Washbrook, D.A. *The Emergence of Provincial Politics: The Madras Presidency 1870–1920*. Cambridge: Cambridge University Press, 1976.

Winge, Glenn Max. *Philosophies of Education: An Introduction*. Delhi: Sterling Publishers, 1975.

Wirth, A.G. *John Dewey as Educator*. New York: John Wiley & Sons, 1966.

Wright, Nigel. *Progress in Education*. London: Croom Helm, 1977.

Zaidi, S.K. 'Basic Education: A Critique'. *New Age*, February 1954.

BOOKS AND ARTICLES IN TAMIL

Anaimuthu, V., ed. *Periyar E.Ve.Ra. Chinthanaigal.* 3 vols. Tiruchi: Thinkers Forum, 1974.

Annadurai, C.N. *Varnasharamam.* Thuraiyur: Dravida Pannai, 1952.

Arunan, S. *Dravida Iyakkam: Oru Marxia Aaivu.* Madurai, 1981.

Ayyamuthu, Kovai. *Rajaji: En Thanthai.* Singarampalayam: Printed by author, 1970.

Chittrarasu, C.P. *Dr Varadarajulu Naidu Vazhkai Varalaru.* Madras: Association Publishing House, 1957.

Chockalingam, T.S. *Kamaraj.* Madras: Navayuga Prachuralayam, 1955.

———. *Enadu Muthal Sandhippu.* Tiruchi: Palaniappa Bros., 1956.

Ganesan, P.C. *Bharatha Perum Thalaivar Kamaraj.* Madras: Arunodayam Press, 1975.

Ilamurugu Porchelvi, Mee. Su. *Aadum Achariar.* Tiruchi: Namnattu Pannai, 1954.

Kamala, V.S. *Thalaivar Sathyamurthi.* Madras: Lalitha Vilasa Puthagasalai, 1967.

Karunanandham. *Thanthai Periyar.* Madras: Printed by author, 1979.

Maraimalayan. *Perarignar Annavin Peruvazhvu.* Madras: Vanathi Pathippagam, 1978.

Muthusami, Mu. Ka. *Arignar Anna Vazhkai Varalaru.* Madras: Satya Pathippagam.

Duraikkannan, Narana. *Rajaji Charitham.* Chennai: Sakthi Publishing House, 1938.

———. *Rajaji.* Madras: Alliance Company, 1948.

Parthasarathy, T.M. *Ti.Mu.Ka. Varalaru.* Madras: Pari Nilayam, 1961.

Ramamurthi, P. Review of *Dravida Iyakkam: Oru Marxia Aaivu*, by S. Arunan. Serialized in *Theekathir*, 1981.

Ramasamy, Periyar E. Ve. *Achariar Atchiyin Kodumaigal.* Erode: Kudiarasu Press,1954.

Santhanalakshmi, S. *Kamaraj.* Tiruchi: Palaniappa Bros., 1975.

Sundaravadivelu, Ne. Du. *Puratchiyalar Periyar.* Madras: S. Chand & Co., 1979.

Vanjikovan, Ma. Ra. *Perarignar Anna Vazhkai Varalaru.* Madras: Balasaraswathi Book Depot, 1970.

Viswanathan, Seeni. *Bharatha Ratna Rajaji.* Madras: Sri Bhuvaneshwari Pathippagam, 1980.

INTERVIEWS

M. Bhaktavatsalam, Chief Minister of Tamil Nadu (1963–67)

Rajmohan Gandhi, biographer of Rajaji

N.D. Sundaravadivelu, Director of Public Instruction (1954–69) and Vice-Chancellor of Madras University (1969–75)

C. Subramaniam, Minister of Finance and Education (in the Rajaji and Kamaraj ministries)

P. Ramamurthi, Deputy Leader of Opposition in 1952–54, Communist Party of India (Marxist)

L.N. Gopalaswami, Thakkar Baba Nilayam, Madras, close associate of Rajaji

UNPUBLISHED THESES

Sivakami, Aruna. 'Rajaji: A Study in Politics and Administration'. PhD diss., University of Madras, 1980.

Lalithalakshmi, S. 'Kamaraj as Administrator'. PhD diss., University of Madras, 1981.

Swaminathan, Saroja. 'S. Sathyamurthi: Political Biography'. PhD diss., University of Madras, 1981.

Shanmugaswami, R. 'Indian National Movement and S. Satyamurthi'. PhD diss., University of Madras, 1977.

Kalaimani, M. 'Periyarum Iyakkangalum'. MPhil diss., University of Madras, 1980.

Muthusami, A. 'Periyarum Arasiyalum: Oru Aaivu'. MPhil diss., University of Madras, 1980.

NEWSPAPERS AND MAGAZINES: ENGLISH

Eastern Economist

Economic & Political Weekly

Educational India

Harijan

The Hindu, Madras

Madras Information

New Age

Pacific Affairs

Social Scientist

The South Indian Teacher

Swatantra

NEWSPAPERS AND MAGAZINES: TAMIL

Ananda Vikatan

Dravida Nadu

Janasakthi

Kalki

Kudi Arasu

Manram

Theekathir

Viduthalai

INDEX

Adams, William
  education in mid-19th-century India 76
Adiseshiah, Malcolm 140, 144
Alagappa Chettiar Committee, the 134–36
  recommendations of 135–36
    implementation of 136–37. *See also* Kamaraj, K.: educational reform under
  Report of 135
Ali, Asaf 32
Ambirajan, S. (IIT Madras professor) 22
  humanities research on interwar period 22–23
Ananda Vikatan (weekly) 122
Andhra Mahasabha conference (1917) 37
Andhra State 59, 111, 115
  demand for 37–38
  formation of 38, 41, 121
    Congress Working Committee recommendation for (1949) 39
    controversy over 39
    impact on Madras Assembly of 41–42, 121–22
    movement for the 39–40
    Rajaji and the 39–40
  Madras city as capital of 40, 121
    Rajaji on 41
Annadurai, C.N. 32, 157
Article 45, of India's Constitution 81, 149
Arumugam, R.S. 105
Arunachalam, K. 134
Arunachalam, M. 134–35, 146
Azad, Abul Kalam 31, 32

Basic Education Scheme, the 48–49, 61, 71–72, 74–75, 79–80, 82, 88–91, 99, 102, 105, 132–33, 135, 138, 145
  components of 42, 90
  J.B. Kripalani's reaction to introduction of 88–89
  Rajaji's differences with 74–75
  schools under 71–72, 82, 85, 134, 135, 136, 138, 146
  socio-economic critique of 145–46
  Zakir Husain Committee Report 42. *See also* Wardha Scheme, the
Bentinck, Lord William 77
Besant, Annie 70
Bharati, Subramania 37
Bhave, Acharya Vinoba 39, 80, 144

Central Advisory Board of Education 131, 151
  opinion on the MSEE 131–32
    Madras government's misrepresentation of 132
Chartists, the 65, 66. *See also* educational reform: in the West
Chengalvarayan, T. 105
Chesneaux, Jean 22
Chettiar, Dr Rm. Alagappa 133
  expert committee under chairmanship of 133. *See also* Alagappa Chettiar Committee, the

Chettiar, M. Singaravelu 21
Chettiar, T.S. Avinashilingam 45, 105
Chockalingam, T.S. 28, 29, 31, 46, 50, 51, 152
Civil Disobedience Movement 30
Commonweal Party 36
Communist Party of India 23, 34, 103, 157
Communist Party of India (Marxist), the 23, 157
  Veeraraghavan's association with 23–24
Compulsory Education Act 138
Constituent Assembly of India 38
Curriculum Revision Committee 130. *See also* Parulekar Committee, the: Report of, the

Dewey, John 53, 64, 65, 155, 156. *See also* educational reform: in the West
Dey, Dr B.B. 116. *See also* Parulekar Committee, the: composition of, the
Dharmalingam, M. 104
Dhar, S.K. 38
  commission for linguistic reorganization of provinces 38
District Teachers' Guild of South Arcot 96
Dravida Munnetra Kazhagam, the 48–49, 53–54, 101–3, 109–11, 113, 125–27
  change in character of 127
  mummunai porattam (three-pronged agitation) of 49, 111
Dravidar Kazhagam 47, 54, 101, 103, 109–11, 113, 124–25
  agitation against MSEE 110–11
  Viduthalai (daily) 47, 101–2
    1953 cartoon from 108, 110
    criticism of MSEE 101–2
    Gurusamy, Kuthoosi (managing editor) 47
Du Bois, W.E.B. 65, 72, 152. *See also* educational reform: in the West; *See also* educational reform: for American Blacks
Dutt, Romesh Chandra 69

Eastern Economist (newspaper) 129
East India Company 37, 76. *See also* educational reform: in India: Charter Act of 1813
  Anglicists, the 77. *See also* educational reform: in India: decline of indigenous schools
educational reform
  for American Blacks 65, 72
  in India 69–70
    beginnings of 69
    British objective of 68
    Charter Act of 1813 76
    decline of indigenous schools 77
    impact of 1937 Congress victory on 79
    Sargent Scheme 80
    shift system 94
      recommendations for a 80
    universal elementary education 59, 69, 78–81
      1910 resolution by Gokhale in Imperial Legislative Assembly for 78
      deterrents to 78, 80–81
      Rajaji's views on 81
  in Tamil Nadu 83
    shift system, the 43, 45, 79, 82, 99
      in the MSEE 85
      Rajaji on 81
      revival by Kamaraj of 137. *See also* Kamaraj, K.: educa-

tional reform under
universal elementary
education 81, 99, 137.
See also Kamaraj, K.: educational reform under
in the West 61–66
education in 19th-century India 76

Fellenberg, Emanuel 63. *See also* educational reform: in the West
Froebel, Friedrich 64. *See also* educational reform: in the West

Gadgil, Professor N.V. 100. *See also* Modified Scheme of Elementary Education, the: support for
Gaekwad of Baroda, the 78. *See also* educational reform: in India: universal elementary education
Gandhigram Rural Institute 91
Gandhi, Indira 52, 53
Gandhi, M.K. 12–13, 20, 29, 31–33, 35, 41–42, 50, 54, 58, 61, 64–65, 67, 70–75, 79, 92, 145–46
charkha 12, 71
educational philosophy of 71–72
support of industrialists to the 72
Gandhi Ashram (Tiruchengode) 32
Harijan (newspaper) 33, 71
Khadi 71
seeds of educational philosophy of 64, 67
socio-economic philosophy of 71
Gandhi, Rajmohan 29, 31, 35, 41, 157
Ghose, Aurobindo 70
Gokhale, G.K. 69, 78–79
Gopalan, K.P.R. 112
Government of India Act of 1935 13, 30, 42, 78
Gowd, H. Siddanna 112. *See also* Modified Scheme of Elementary Education, the: discussions in the Assembly on

Harijan Welfare Schools 138
Husain, Zakir 91, 106, 116

Indian National Congress, the 13, 78
demand for linguistic provinces 38
in Tamil Nadu 27–28, 30, 32, 121–23, 124–26, 133
de-Brahminization of 27–28, 126–27
in 1952 election 34
Karachi session (1931) 78. *See also* educational reform: in India: universal elementary education
Linguistic Provinces Committee (Jaipur session, 1948) 38
Rajaji's position in 30–32
Indian Socialist Party 103
International Labour Organization 101
Iyengar, Krishnaswamy 44. *See also* Modified Scheme of Elementary Education, the: first trial in Periyakulam of (1937)
Iyengar, N. Kuppuswamy 92, 94–95
Iyer, G. Subramania 27
Iyer, V.R. Krishna 129

Justice Party 28, 30, 153–55. *See also* Non-Brahmin Manifesto (December 1916): South Indian Liberal Federation

Kamaraj, K. 27–35, 46–47, 50–53, 59, 104, 121–27, 133–34, 136–39, 142, 150
educational reform under 136–39

analysis of 139–44, 150
K Plan of 52, 126
rise of 27, 30–31, 52–53, 123–24
the Kingmaker 33
taking over as Chief Minister 133
Kannan, S.S. 17, 20, 24–25
Kosalram, K.T. 50, 122–24
Krishnamurthy, C. 80
Krishnamurthy, Kalki R. 18, 29, 35, 51, 87, 89, 107
Kalki (weekly) 18, 107, 122
1953 cartoon from 52, 119
support for MSEE 107–8
Kumarappa, J.C. 91, 93, 154
Kumaraswamy Raja, P.S. 33–35, 39
Kurien, C.T. 144

Lakshmipathi, Dr A. 75

Macaulay, Thomas Babington 68, 77
Madras Educational Rules, the weakening of 131
Madras State
Education Department 46, 58, 75, 77, 84, 90, 99, 107–8, 150–51
objections to MSEE 84
Malabar Elementary School Teachers' Union 89
Ma.Po.Si. *See* Sivagnanam, M.P.
Marx, Karl 24, 66–67, 154
on education 66
Menon, Dr K.B. 88, 103
Minimum Age (Agriculture) Convention, 1921 100
Modified Scheme of Elementary Education, the 17–18, 27, 48, 54, 57, 76, 87, 97, 111, 115, 118, 123, 129, 132, 136, 139, 149–50
and Kamaraj 51, 104
announcement of intention for 43
initial reaction to 83
announcement of
reactions to the 45–46, 87–88, 89–96
by the Opposition 88
story of the 44–45
craft training under 85–86, 93
arguments against 93–94
criticism of
by educationists 90–96
by Periyar 49
by the CPI 103
by the Indian Socialist Party 103–4
by the Toilers' Party 104
government response to 106–9
in *Viduthalai* 101–2
differences with Basic Education 91
discussions in the Assembly on 111–13
Rajaji's stance during 112, 115
education in Madras State before 43
first trial in Periyakulam of (1937) 44, 75
failure of the 75
impact on teachers 89–90
initial justification for 86–87
feared impact on students 92–93
opposition to
'kula kalvi thittam' 22, 27, 57, 102
'protest day' against 109
Rajaji on the 123
within the INC 104–5
proposals of 57, 85–86
revised pupil–teacher ratio (1954) 90
shift system in 85, 92–93
arguments against 94, 105
socio-economic critique of 95–96,

100–1, 146–47
support for 91, 96–100
arguments in 97
undemocratic introduction of 46–48, 84, 87–88, 150
withdrawal of 133
Rajaji's response to 134
Montagu–Chelmsford reforms 70, 78
Montessori, Madame Maria 70
Mudaliar, Dr A. Lakshmanaswami 99
Mudaliar, Thiru. Vi. Kalyanasundara 28, 35
Mujeeb, M. (VC, JMI) 116. *See also* Parulekar Committee, the: composition of, the
Myrdal, Gunnar 72

Nagarajan, V.R. 104, 116
Naicker, Manickavelu 36
Naidu, Nathamuni 47
Naidu, P. Varadarajulu 28, 50, 122, 127, 157
Naidu, Rajaram 102
Naidu, Santhana Krishna 99. *See also* Modified Scheme of Elementary Education, the: support for
Naidu, S. Govindarajulu (DPI) 41, 43–45, 47, 84, 116
Naik, J.P. 80, 155
Nambiar, T.C. Narayana 89–90, 116, 130
Naoroji, Dadabhai 69
Natarajan, S. 89, 93. *See also* South India Teachers' Union
National Education Movement 69, 70, 78
National University (1918) 70. *See also* educational reform: in India
Nayagar, A. Govindaswami 104, 116
Nehru, Jawaharlal 30, 38–39, 122, 145
economic development under 145–46
Non-Brahmin Manifesto (December 1916)
South Indian Liberal Federation 28
Non-Cooperation movement (1921) 30, 70–71
Non-Formal System of Education 144
North Arcot District Educational Conference 47
Sundaravadivelu speaks at 47

Owen, Robert 66. *See also* educational reform: in the West

Pal, T.V.G. 99
panchayats 67, 107, 109
Parulekar Committee, the 59, 81, 90, 101, 117, 120, 129–32, 137
composition of, the 115–16
criticism of 116
government's defence of 116–17
Kamaraj government's implementation of pupil–teacher ratio recommended by 137
Report of, the 59, 82, 101, 107, 117–18, 121, 129–31
conclusions and recommendations 118–20, 130
implementation of 120, 130–31, 137
methodology of 117
submission of 117
Parulekar, Ramchandra Vithal 79–80, 115
ideas on primary education 79
Patel, Vallabhbhai 34, 38
Paul, Lt. Col. S. (Principal, Guindy Engineering College) 99. *See also* Modified Scheme of Elementary Education, the: support for
Periyar E.V. Ramasamy 28, 30, 47–50,

75–76, 101–2, 111, 127, 133
criticism of Basic Education Scheme 48–49
pro-Kamarajism of 127
resisting the MSEE 49, 102
Self-Respect Movement 28, 30, 154
Pestalozzi, Johann Heinrich 63, 92. *See also* educational reform: in the West
Leonard and Gertrude 63
Pillai, S.C.C. Anthony 88, 104
Post-War Reconstruction Committee for Educational Development 80
Prakasam, T. 33–35, 38–40, 83, 112, 121, 138

Quit India Movement, the 31–32, 126
Rajaji and 31

Rajagopalachari, C. 11–12, 14–15, 19, 22, 26–36, 38–51, 53–54, 55–59, 61, 64, 73–76, 80–81, 83–84, 87–88, 91–92, 95–99, 101–3, 105–13, 115–17, 120–27, 129, 132–34, 136, 139, 144–47, 149–50, 152
after the elections in 1952 13
allegation of casteism against 103
anti-Non-Brahmin acts of 102
as national leader 34
as Premier of Madras State 30–31
Chief Minister, the 83
achievements as 36–37, 125
on becoming 35–36, 83
concessions on the MSEE 106–7, 109, 116
decline within INC 31, 124–26
early life 12–13, 29
educational philosophy of 73–74
European influence on educational philosophy of 64
Gandhi's conscience keeper 29
high-handedness of 14–15, 124
opposition within INC to 122–24
resignation of 51, 123, 133
return to INC in 1945 31–32
Swatantra Party 49, 51, 73, 125
tiff with T. Prakasam 35
Rajah, H.D. 100. *See also* Modified Scheme of Elementary Education, the: support for
Rajaji. *See* Rajagopalachari, C.
Rajaji–Kamaraj alliance (1971) 53
Rajaji–Kamaraj rivalry 32–33, 123
Gandhi's visit to Chennai in 1946 32–33
Rajaji–Periyar public appearance (1953) 49–50
Ramachandran, G. 91, 96–99, 105, 120. *See also* Modified Scheme of Elementary Education, the: support for
Ramamurthi, P. 21, 23, 88, 103
Ranade, M.G. 69
Rao, Dr M.V. Krishna 41, 45, 83, 88
Rathinam, A. 104
Reddiar, Omandur P. Ramaswamy 33, 45, 82, 104, 137
Reddy, Dr Muthulakshmi 100. *See also* Modified Scheme of Elementary Education, the: support for
Reddy, T. Nagi 88, 103, 112
Robinson Crusoe 62
Rousseau, Jean-Jacques 53, 62–63, 99, 152. *See also* educational reform: in the West
Emile (1762) 62–63

Sabanayagam, P. (Rajaji's private secretary) 46, 47
Salem Dravidian Teachers' Union 102
Sambamurthy, Bulusu 40
Sastri, K.S. Ramaswami 99

Sathyagangai (newspaper) 44
Satyamurti, S. 30
School Improvement Scheme 139. *See also* Kamaraj, K.: educational reform under
Sen, Amartya 143
Shastri, Lal Bahadur 52
Sitaramayya, Pattabhi 38
Sivagnanam, M.P. 29, 51. *See also* Indian National Congress, the: in Tamil Nadu: Tamilarasu Kazhagam
Sivasami, K.C. 100. *See also* Modified Scheme of Elementary Education, the: support for
South India Teachers' Union 87, 89, 92–93, 96, 129, 131
  reaction to introduction of MSEE 87, 89, 96
  The South Indian Teacher (journal) 92
Spencer, Herbert 53, 64. *See also* educational reform: in the West
Srinivasa Iyengar, R. 70, 74, 82, 89, 91–92, 95–96, 130
Srinivasan, Saraswathy 96
Srinivasaraghavan, A. (Principal, V.O.C. College, Tuticorin) 100. *See also* Modified Scheme of Elementary Education, the: support for
Sriramulu, Potti 39, 40. *See also* Andhra State: formation of: movement for the
Sriram, V. (music historian) 24
Statham, R.M. (DPI) 44, 74–75, 80
Subbarayan, Dr P. 105
Subramaniam, C. 18, 33, 41, 46, 48, 84, 106, 112, 115–16, 124, 129, 132, 133
  becomes Education Minister 41
Subramaniam, C.S. 21–22
Sundaravadivelu, N.D. (Dy DPI) 18, 43–48, 75–76, 82, 84, 134
  endorses the MSEE 47
  memoirs of 44
Swadharma (journal of labour issues) 21
Swatantra (newspaper) 129

Tagore, Rabindranath 70, 73
Tamilarasu Kazhagam 51
Tamil Nadu Congress Committee, the 30, 32, 58, 105, 122–23, 151
  Rajaji's election to 32
Tamil Nadu State Planning Commission 141, 143, 151
Tamil Nadu Toilers' Party 104, 112
Thangavelu, S.P. 104
The Hindu 21, 45, 134
The Indian Express 45
Thiru.Vi.Ka. *See* Mudaliar, Thiru. Vi. Kalyanasundara
Thompson, E.P. 22
Tilak, Bal Gangadhar 29, 69–70
Tiruchi Taluk Dravidian Agricultural Workers Conference 102
Tiruvalluvar 107

United Democratic Front 34, 104, 121
Unnithan, K.M. (education secretary, Madras) 45

Vaikom Satyagraha (1924) 30
Vanniya Kula Kshatriya Sangam 127
varnashrama dharma 71, 73, 76, 102, 125
Vedanta Desikar 107
Vedic Age, the 61
Veeraraghavan, D. 13–15, 17–19, 21–26, 36, 41–44, 46, 48–50, 53–54, 121
  loss of vision 23
  published works of 25–26

The Making of the Madras Working Class 19, 21, 25
writing of 21–22
weaknesses in analysis of 54
Veerasami, V. 110
Venkatachalam, Jothi 122
Venkatarangaiah, Professor M. 100. *See also* Modified Scheme of Elementary Education, the: support for
village economy in India, the
British impact on 67–68, 77–78
Viswanatham, Tenneti 38–39, 88, 104, 112
Viswanathan, K.R. 112
Vyapuri, A. 101. *See also* Salem Dravidian Teachers' Union

Wanchoo, K.N. 40
report on Andhra State formation of committee headed by 40–41
Wardha Scheme, the 42, 48, 75. *See also* Basic Education Scheme, the
Wood's Despatch of 1854 78